To Mum, Dad,
Ronan, Laura, Julie, Andrea and Billy

Contents

Prologue

March, 2012

IT WAS AS IF IT had been lying in wait, ready to pounce when the opportunity presented. For days before *The Voice* live shows I walked around with a mounting discomfort, beginning in the pit of my stomach, rising into my throat and leaving me short of breath, while at night, my thoughts rushed so fast I couldn't sleep. I didn't have much experience of television so I put my unease down to performance anxiety. When my legs came from underneath me inside the dressing room just minutes before we were due to go live, and my breath stopped coming, I knew this was panic at its worst.

For many years I'd struggled with attacks of this kind, as part of a condition I have called generalised anxiety disorder, but it wasn't ever something I talked about. Not even those closest to me knew the extent of my condition, and I had been fiercely protective in my efforts to hide this part of my life from everyone around me.

Curled on the floor in the private confines of the dressing room, gripped by overwhelming fear, time seemed to come to a halt and when I willed myself back to reality, I moved through slow motion. I could hear the sound engineer rapping on the door, ever increasingly as the minutes to transmission ticked by. I tried to call out but not a sound came, it seemed nothing could pull me back as I folded up tighter, breathless, choked and apoplectic with terror.

I didn't know how I could survive this one, punching my chest to try to find a breath, pulling my shirt until it tore. But in the midst of this madness, something new became clear to me. I knew that if I got past tonight, I could not go on like this. Something had to give. The secret I had kept for years and guarded with all my life for fear of stigma and alienation could not remain secret for much longer.

1. The Holy Land

I WAS BROUGHT UP IN Mullingar, a rural, regional midlands town, by an army officer father and a music teacher mother. Nothing existed or mattered outside my town. It was the centre of the earth. I got a nose bleed if I went past Kinnegad on the N4, and a holiday meant being dragged to Dublin Zoo in the depths of winter for a school trip, or if you were feeling really adventurous, an expedition to the Natural History Museum, followed by a Happy Meal in McDonald's. I am not saying I was sheltered, but I certainly wasn't Phileas Fogg. So when my parents informed me that we were going to move to Israel for an extended period of time I thought to myself, whereabouts in Dublin is Israel?

My dad was often stationed overseas for up to a year at a time, when the Irish army were sent to work as peacekeepers for the United Nations. I vividly remember as a child being woken in the middle of the night along with my brother and three sisters, to say goodbye to him. He would be collected in an army van at dawn, and

I would watch him break down into tears before having to leave his wife and kids and go to often hostile and dangerous countries. Watching my father cry had quite a profound impact on me. Dad would always assure me that wherever he was going was safe, but seeing this strong and powerful figure in my life become vulnerable and emotionally volatile stirred a sense of insecurity in my otherwise blissfully ignorant and carefree existence. I used to ask my father to say goodbye to me before I went to sleep so I would not have to be part of these nocturnal goodbyes. As he would leave in the early hours, I would pretend I was asleep and put the pillow over my ears so I would not hear the door shut behind him. I would then come downstairs and try to support my mother, a calm, creative and beautiful Glaswegian woman.

Only as I grew older could I make sense of this. The sadness of a father having to say goodbye to the people he loved the most in this world, and miss a year of their journey through life. I am not a father but I can still empathise with how incredibly challenging emotionally this must have been, not just for my father, but for his wife, my mother.

My father had to go overseas so often that it was a welcome opportunity when he was in a position to invite his family to spend a portion of his duty with him. I had just turned 12 when he was stationed in Southern Lebanon with the United Nations Interim Force in Lebanon, and we were to join him for a number of months. As it was still a relatively unstable environment we decided we would stay in Nahariya, a sleepy coastal town just inside Israel on the border with Lebanon, and about a 45-minute drive from the camp where Dad worked.

So on 14 May 1993, my family and I departed the centre of the earth and began our exciting quest to the Holy Land. I had just left primary school, and left behind that jittery time when you establish who your friends are going to be in secondary school. Who was I going to hang around with in Israel? My older brother had decided to stay behind. The two older girls were hardly going to hang around with their teenage brother, and my younger sister and I were engaged in some pretty animated rows. But there was no choice but to go, and I was a curious kid, fascinated by new places and people. My father was already in Israel preparing the town for the onslaught of the Breslins.

I distinctly recall the flight from London Heathrow to Tel Aviv Ben Gurion International Airport. Going through airport security with our enormous suitcases, I was amazed at the extent of the security operations, as military men body-scanned and searched us. I was very innocent about the conflict going on in Israel, and thought I could just breeze onto the plane. I hadn't realised a 13-year-old with a rucksack from the midlands could be a potential security threat entering the Middle East. On the plane, we made our way to the smoking section where my mum, a smoker at the time, had slyly booked our seats. I had just settled into my seat for the five-hour journey when I was asked by the flight attendant, who was robbed of any personality or patience (especially for an overzealous Irish kid pepped up on duty-free Haribo Bears and Toblerone) would I mind moving to the front of the plane to let a smoker sit in my seat. She more demanded than asked, but either way I found myself sitting alone, beside two Orthodox Jews who seemed rather disconcerted that some sour-faced teenager was occupying the seat next to them. I was more perplexed by the fact that they were wearing long black dresses and oversized bowler hats. I quietly cursed the smoker that had me pulled from the pleasant fog of the smoking section. About an hour into the flight one of the men beside me fell into a deep sleep. His head gradually started tilting towards my shoulder and I knew what was going to happen next.

Here I was, away from the comfort of my mother, with some random chap drooling on my shoulder in the depths of sleep while my sugar buzz faded. I missed Mullingar. I was praying for turbulence so he would be jolted from his slumber and I could have my saliva-stained shoulder back. Luckily as the food was being served the odour of the delight that is airline cuisine hit his senses and he woke, oblivious to the fact that he had used me as a human pillow for the previous two hours. As he was eating his breakfast, I informed him that I liked his hat and dress. I was completely naive to the culture I was about to spend the coming months in, its religious and ethnic divisions. He smiled and asked me where I was from. I told him I was Irish and was going over to live with my dad who was stationed in the Lebanon. In a very considerate tone, without condescending to me, he then explained the fundamentals of the history of Israel and his religion. I was like a sponge. He explained to me his beliefs, and I informed him of mine, Christian, the single belief system I was aware of. He also educated me on the hostilities and complexities of the situation in the Middle East, and I thought to myself, why are my parents bringing us here? I told him that where I was from, the only hostilities we ever witnessed were when some lad annoyed you in school and you hit him a box.

When we landed in Tel Aviv I was so thankful I hadn't had to choke down in the smoking section and also that I got to learn quite a lot about this intriguing but complicated country. We disembarked just as the sun was rising, and already the intense heat I'd been warned about hit my face like I had just opened an oven. All my family had managed to sleep on the flight but because I was burning the ear off my Jewish friend for the entire flight, I did not sleep a wink. It started to catch up with me as we dragged ourselves through the airport and waited for our luggage. I was like Damien from *The Omen*.

As we came through the arrivals gate, my father was waiting, palpably excited to see us. Unusually for him, he wasn't in uniform that day. You could see the relief on his face that we actually made it to Israel. It was an emotional moment, and the polar opposite to the early-hour tearful goodbyes I so hated. I was just about sleepwalking by the time we made our way to the United Nations minivan dad had borrowed to pick us up. Nahariya was about a two-hour drive north. Sitting in between my sisters on burning hot leather seats I peered out the windows, mesmerised by the scenery, the absolute beauty of this desert landscape. It was a far cry from the N4 to Dublin.

Driving into Nahariya I half expected to see a town wounded by the legacy of warfare and conflict, but what I witnessed was a charming coastal region that was modernised and, surprisingly, quite normal. We pulled up to our new home for the foreseeable future, a high-rise apartment block that looked like it had been built in rebellion to elegance, or as my mother called it, 'practical'. A nice way of saying it was a shithole. Myself and my sisters tore each other to shreds trying to get through the front door to mark our territory and claim the more appealing bedroom. I lost the battle and ended up in a tiny room I would share with my younger sister, Andrea. At this stage the heat of the early-morning sun was sweltering through the windows of our first floor apartment and I was immensely eager to explore my new surroundings. Through the midst of exhaustion I was excited to discover the unfamiliar world I now found myself in.

Aesthetically, the town was very appealing and with miles of beach surrounding it, it almost felt like paradise. However, there was a tangible tension in the air, an underlying unease that was hard to ignore. Young adult men and women walked around with semi-automatic weapons, dressed in full military attire. The war ships were anchored menacingly in the bay, while Apache helicopters patrolled the skies above us. I looked for constant reassurance from my mother, who was sure to offer it every time. But no doubt about it, I was slightly shaken.

The first few weeks in Israel were a steep learning curve of cultural confusion combined with an internal uneasiness that was an entirely new experience for me. One morning my father brought us over the border into Southern Lebanon to visit his camp and to shop on the run-down thoroughfare that was aptly called Mingy Street. It was a street where you could buy cheap knock-off goods, with deep baskets of fake Nike, Adidas and Reebok runners, fake designer clothes on rails right onto the street, and boxes filled with pirated cassette tapes. The street had been badly bombed by the Israeli Defence Force (IDF), with some of the shops blown down at the side. Their walls were riddled with bullet holes, which I rushed to, putting my index finger into the holes to see if they could be real. I filled my arms with pirated tapes and pleaded with my parents for more dollars; I had my heart set on a pair of Reebok pumps which were huge at the time but way outside the price range of most teenagers. I got myself a pair for $30 on Mingy Street, delighted with myself. Back outside I wondered what the war ships were doing, bobbing on the water. Apart from its air of menace, the coastline had an untainted beauty that reminded me of West Cork.

Although Nahariya was only 20 miles south, it did not bear a remote resemblance to the towns and villages in Southern Lebanon. The years of conflict and war in this region were clearly evident in the craters in the ground left by the air strikes, in the derelict houses half standing, in the landmine warnings on the verges of every road, and the burnt-out cars and tanks lining the fields. When we were out for dinner, we got used to the sight of soldiers swaggering through the doors with guns slung over their shoulders. Sometimes I joined a group of soldiers playing five-a-side football on the beach, still on duty with their weapons slung about them. I learned not to throw a dirty tackle when there was a guy with an M16 around his shoulder – though unfortunately in later life, such caution wouldn't serve me. One day, going into a shopping centre with my parents, we discovered there had been a bomb threat inside, and the whole town was shut down by the army. We found out later the device had been real, defused just in time. The people lived in constant fear of retaliation attacks between the Israeli Defence Force and Hezbollah, an organisation with its roots in Lebanon. What a beautiful, troubled region, I thought, with a dark shadow of fear and tension lurking over its landscape.

I was finally beginning to settle in to our new home, when one night I was woken by a lady jabbering into a loudspeaker outside the block of apartments. She was a soldier, I gathered, speaking in broken English as she ordered all residents to vacate their homes and make their way into the bomb shelters situated in the basement of the apartment. At first I thought I was dreaming and brushed it off, until my sisters came into the room to get me out of bed. I knew it was serious, because nothing other than an emergency could get my sisters out of bed. My parents seemed to be downplaying the situation as my dad then appeared at the bedroom door, telling me it was a relatively normal occurrence. I wasn't to be afraid, he said. We decided to stay in the apartment and I was encouraged to try to go back to sleep. Hold on a second here, go back to sleep? Two minutes ago some lady was roaring through a loudspeaker to get into the bomb shelters, and now my mum was telling me to try to get some sleep? I wasn't buying it.

I lay awake for the next three or four hours feeling deeply confused and strangely nauseated. When you're physically sick, you find a position in your bed where you are comfortable but I couldn't find comfort anywhere. I can safely say that this was my initial introduction to anxiety. I felt so exposed to danger. For the first time in my life, the invincibility that I courted through my early years was robbed from me.

The next morning at breakfast I quizzed my father on what had happened. He told me that Hezbollah had begun shelling northern Israel but that I wasn't to worry, as they only had two types of missiles. One that could not reach us, and the other one that would go over our heads. Oh, well, that's grand so, stuck in no man's land hoping the missiles land where they are supposed to. I was greatly confused. On the news that morning we heard that the Israeli Defence Force had begun retaliation proceedings in Southern Lebanon, naming the mission 'Operation Accountability', marking the commencement of the 1993 conflict between the IDF and Hezbollah in which countless civilians lost their lives. In our 'practical' tower block in the heart of Nahariya, my family and I found ourselves stuck in the middle of an army campaign. I grew to hate that apartment. Its roaming cockroaches and the cold, sterile tiles, and the boredom of turning on the TV to remember that, yes, everything was in Hebrew.

We lived for five months in the Holy Land, though not long enough for me to attend school. After the retaliation began, every day we would feel the ground vibrate viciously as the Israeli Air Force relentlessly bombarded targets in Southern Lebanon just a few miles north from where we were staying. You could clearly hear the powerful explosions and the snaps of gunfire. One day the windows of our apartment began violently shaking while the walls began swaying, and I thought, either we've been hit with a missile, or this is an earthquake. It turned out to be a sonic boom from one of the Israeli Air Force jets passing overhead. Sonic booms occur when the jet breaks the speed of sound and causes shock waves that affect the areas below the aircraft, I learned, though it gave me no pleasure to receive this information.

I had felt nauseous in my bed the night we were ordered into the bomb shelters; now, I felt sick to the pit of my stomach with worry, not just for my own safety but for my father's safety. Every day he was travelling up to the border and into his base camp in Southern Lebanon, and I used to fear he wouldn't come back. Every night I would lie wide awake, feeling the weight of something pressing on my chest. I was becoming suffocated with nerves. Sometimes, I would drag my mattress to the door of my parents' bedroom in the middle of the night as I felt a little safer when I was closer to the two of them.

This relentless unrest was a new experience for me. No longer was I a carefree, sociable and adventurous kid, and I hated the realisation that my youthful invincibility had turned to deep insecurity, and to existing constantly on edge.

But in many ways teenage life went on as normal. I had my first real growth spurt when I was in Israel. I went from being a chubby, slightly uncoordinated, awkward kid, to being six foot in what felt like overnight. I inherited my height from my mum's late father, my Glaswegian grandfather 'Bumper', a six-foot-six juggernaut and a devout Celtic fan. Gaining ground like this was, I guess, the beginning of my lifelong love of sport. In the dry heat of Nahariya I started playing basketball, football and tennis, often with the Irish soldiers. I was comforted in the realisation that sport and physical activity could momentarily mask my worries and anxieties, something that has served me fruitfully throughout my life – though at times with mixed results. And despite my perpetual state of distress, I started to emerge from my shell.

I liked hanging around the kibbutz where my sister went to live and farm the land. I liked the wreck houses on the beach where the military and their ex-pat families came to eat dinner and have a drink at the bar, because there I discovered the delights of entertaining people. On 'Irish nights' I'd step in as DJ, putting my illegal cassettes from Mingy Street into a dated stereo in the wreck house. At the time, 'Informer' by Snow was the big hit, and I continuously played the song trying to figure out what the hell he was rapping about. I never did figure it out. The United Nations families did not share my fascination with that tune and it was quickly banned from the playlist.

Israel opened my eyes and my mind. I travelled to incredible places like the West Bank, Gaza, the Dead Sea and Jerusalem. There was a world beyond the boundaries of Mullingar. A world so unstable and complicated. A world where war and conflict were part of daily routine. I feel privileged to have had my eyes opened at such a young age. Although it may have put an end to my youthful innocence and marked the birth of my anxiety, it educated me in ways no teacher or school could do. It ignited curiosities and made me appreciate the comfort of my hometown and the fact that I was born and able to live in a country where I didn't have to fear for my life, or the lives of my family.

2. Teenage kicks

I RETURNED FROM ISRAEL A different person, physically and mentally. Mullingar seemed like such a different place yet nothing had changed, I was the one who had changed. Disproportionately tall and particularly awkward, I felt like an imposter. My friends and classmates barely recognised me. I barely recognised their new identities. In my absence, they had discovered the appeal of the opposite sex, the possibilities of drinking and stealing smokes. Much of their conversation now revolved around getting the shift and fictional stories of awkward sexual experiences, whereas before, it was about football and the price of Mr Freezes. Socially, I found myself isolated and unable to relate to their interests. I felt they were trivial and infantile compared to what I had been exposed to over the previous months. This town that I had thought was the centre of the earth almost became a source of personal resentment, for its simple perception of everything that existed outside its claustrophobic grasp. It seemed like nothing else mattered outside this town to these people. But I had grown too fast, been exposed to too much. Everything I'd heard and seen I'd taken on in my mind and heart and gripped onto. I felt paranoid among friends and ultimately decided there was more comfort in being alone.

After school, I used to strategically map my journey home so as to avoid any possibility of coming into contact with friends or classmates. When I got home I would invent elaborate excuses as to why I did not want to go out and socialise with my friends, and if they knocked on the front door I would get my mother to tell them I wasn't around. Israel had brought me closer to my mother, and I knew she would cover for me. For a 13-year-old, it really should be the other way around – pleading with your mother to let you out of the house. I rebelled against my own extrovert nature and developed into a painfully reclusive character. I would make up stories about my friends and embellish their bad sides to justify to myself why I had disowned them. I distorted in my mind the characters of my friends, just to keep as far away as possible.

I could not make sense of this polar transformation in my character, and as each day went by I grew more and more frustrated with the seeming lack of control I had in reversing it. Of course, puberty had its part to play in my moody state, but I felt its contribution was relatively secondary to something a little more nocuous. Being alone so much, I knew this behaviour was not sustainable nor was it healthy. It was having a profoundly negative impact on my self-esteem and confidence. I felt ashamed and embarrassed, completely unable to understand or rationalise my own behaviour.

For Christmas that year my parents bought me a cheap electric guitar. I got myself a book of guitar chords and started to teach myself, spending hours on end in my tiny box room – which I had outgrown, considering I was now the length of the room. I would learn my chords and scales until my fingers literally bled onto the fretboard. There was always music in our house, often coming from the grand piano my grandmother, my mother's mother Granny Mac, left us before she died. Now with my own electric guitar, playing Oasis and Nirvana songs that were so easy to pull off, you felt like a rock star. Every day after school I would climb quickly up to my room, sit on my bed and play along to Green Day and Oasis cassettes as if I was part of their band. I would actually picture myself being out on a stage playing to thousands of people. I created my own little imaginary venue in my room, and managed to occupy hours of the day pretending to play to huge crowds. My guitar became my best friend and that brought me great solace and comfort as I fell deeper into a social Siberia. It still provides that same comfort today, in happier circumstances.

I would spend five or six hours a day in that little bedroom, learning the notes until they were perfect. As isolated and reclusive as I became, I still felt completely content in my own company. Two was a crowd. I always had a vivid imagination and I was able to fabricate situations that made me feel like I was anything from a professional footballer to the best guitarist on the planet.

I would listen to music for hours on end, everything I could find: Pearl Jam, Nirvana, The Red Hot Chili Peppers, Abba; before the heavier days of Faith No More and Metallica kicked in. Bolted into that little room I would sing and play, and when I wasn't being the frontman, I'd imagine myself in the crowd while my favourite band played on stage.

I will never forget the shock of hearing that one of my musical heroes, Kurt Cobain, had taken his life. My sister came upstairs to tell me, 'The guy from Nirvana has been shot.' We rushed to watch the news, where it transpired he'd shot himself, and that he was dead. I couldn't fathom how a man could actually kill himself. I did not have the mental capacity nor maturity to rationalise what had happened. I had never really heard that word before, suicide. I was very curious about why he would have done this. Why would a guy with the biggest band in the world throw it all away? At a time when the majority of my school worshipped Kurt Cobain and Nirvana, it was a pity that our teachers never even mentioned his death. One day a teacher pacing the class saw the words 'RIP Kurt Cobain' carved into a school desk with a compass. 'A shameful and cowardly way to die, and with a wife and child,' I remember him mumbling.

During the summer of 1994, the contentment I enjoyed while alone started showing signs of wear and tear. I became slightly uncomfortable in my own skin. It was as if the vivid imagination I had been blessed with had started to turn on me. My thoughts became irrational and an uneasiness set in when I was alone. Gaining a strong appetite for catastrophe, I made ample room for worries to creep in. My mother had this *Encyclopaedia of Health* that she left on the sitting room table, and I would find myself ensconced at the kitchen table for hours reading it and relating to symptoms of serious physical illnesses. One day I would be convinced I was having an appendicitis attack and my appendix was going to burst, while the next day I would be dying of a brain tumour; I think I was even pregnant at one stage. I began thinking about my mortality, accepting the realisation that we were so exposed and vulnerable to many dangers and threats. Now, I realise I was almost fantasising about my death, entertaining truly morbid worst-case scenarios. The one thing I did suffer from, I didn't look up in this exhaustive volume of diseases. If I'd seen the word anxiety, it wouldn't have meant anything to me. I thought anxiety was just for old people. Or something that happened when you got butterflies in your stomach before a test.

As the months went on, the endless free time of summer holidays became fertile ground for the worst anxieties. At first, I found myself struggling to fall asleep, unable to calm my mind and park these nonsensical thoughts. My body would lie down, my mind would ignite. I was avalanched with a million thoughts a second. I wondered if I would lose my mother or my father, if one of them might die from a terrible illness. I wondered this deep into the night, in blind states of exhaustion. The more I tried to sleep, the less chance I'd get. I would lie in my bed grinding my teeth, irritated with myself for not being able to nod off. I would design problems that did not even exist and dread the following day, when I knew I would be zombie-like with exhaustion.

One warm summer evening in late July, I lay staring at the ceiling in my box room. I could feel my throat starting to close up, as if I had swallowed something and it went down the wrong way. I began frantically thumping my chest to try to relieve this tightness. There was a gut-wrenching pressure in my stomach that led to a cloud of nausea that ached and crippled me. I tried to vomit but I was unable, because I was choking. I fought for breath but it just would not come. I tried to call out but no noise came from my mouth, only the terrifying sound of suffocation, the sound of gasping breath. Tears were streaming down my face, my head was spinning and my heart pounded at the walls of my chest. I was dying. This was it. Game over.

Caught up in a tangled mire of terror within my body, it felt almost as if I'd been possessed. My skin was ghostly white, I could see the veins in my arms swell. Clasping the bed with my shaking fists, head mashed onto the pillow, I went to attempt one last breath. I was in contest with my lungs, which were obstinately closed and out of reach to my feeble respiratory attempts. As I sucked in I managed to catch a tiny bite of air. I could inhale, just the smallest passage of precious air. I felt the pain in my chest ease slightly and soon, gradually, I felt my heart return back to its relatively normal rhythm. I lay face-down on that bed, paralysed with terror and devoid of hope, as whatever demonic spirit had entered now exited my body. Every cell in my body had believed I was going to die. The physical pain in my chest was a reminder of the strange and unbearable experience I had been dragged through, seemingly in slow motion. I had watched plenty of shit horror movies, but seen nothing like this before.

Back then, there was no Google search to find out what the hell had just happened to me. Had there been one, I would not have even known how to explain it in words. I went downstairs and checked the *Encyclopaedia of Health* for any clues. I came across a page on asthma and having read the symptoms, I told myself that I must have asthma, and I had just experienced an asthma attack. I asked my mum whether she thought I had asthma. I didn't tell her precisely what had just happened, because it was too strange, too exhausting to explain. I told her I sometimes have trouble breathing. Concerned, she told me we would keep an eye on it and see if it progressed.

I did not realise it then, but I went to bed that night having experienced my first panic attack. It's a night I will never forget until the day I die. It marked the physical beginning of my journey with anxiety and mental illness. A long road with many twists and turns. A volatile and hostile relationship with the thing that had no name, that ultimately, many years later, I gave a name to, Jeffrey.

The aftershocks of that panic attack arrived, an array of strange new complaints that ensured I would not be able to brush off what had happened. I associated night time and my bed with this horrific experience. I would dread going into my room at night when everyone else was going to sleep. This sanctuary I had been so content and peaceful in became somewhere I feared. It felt like I had nowhere to go. I did not want to socialise with my peers, yet I could not hide in my room and strum guitar and fantasise about playing to thousands anymore. I felt like there was nowhere to go, an utter helplessness. When I lay down flat on my bed, I would immediately feel this rush of panic to my chest, as if a flood was coming and I was drowning. When I closed my eyes I would start sweating from every pore, my heart rate would increase dramatically and I would fight for half a breath. Sleep felt like my enemy and I would lie wide awake at night going through the list of diseases I probably had. Appendicitis, brain cancer, tuberculosis. I became a chronic insomniac, floating into school in a state of confused exhaustion.

Academically, I was reasonably bright, certainly not Stephen Hawking, but well able to apply myself. But now I would fall asleep at my desk in the middle of class, which often brought the wrath of the Christian Brothers' old-fashioned punishment methods on me. One of my major loves, music, was given to me by a Christian Brother so it wasn't all bad, but there were teachers in that school still holding on to the legacy of corporal punishment, who would send a knuckle to the back of your head or a piece of chalk aimed like shrapnel with the precision of William Tell. Their perception of me was no doubt of a lazy, disrespectful waster that was going nowhere in life. Little did they know the acute hell I was staring at, every day. I wonder how much has changed in the education system nowadays, regarding the understanding teachers have of their pupils.

Slowly, the emotional stress I was enduring began manifesting itself physically. I started to lose clumps of hair. I had no appetite. I would often force-feed myself, trying to ignore the constant nauseating pain in my stomach. I would eat packets of cheap crisps and chocolate, anything to give me the energy to stay awake in class. My panic attacks became a lot more frequent. Like a vicious circle, the lack of sleep and exhaustion along with my poor diet led to a breakdown in my immune system, which further led me to believe I was dying of some other disease, which even further translated into nightly terrors and crippling anxiety attacks. The frustration was magnified with each attack and I became so low that I would want, honestly, to tear my own skin off. Every inch of my character was being slowly shredded within me and I felt soulless and completely alone. Nowadays, I always think to myself, imagine if I was from a dysfunctional family or had other social pressures, like being bullied at school, compounding these issues I dealt with. Could I have survived? Of course we all can survive, but having a loving and stable family was, at the time, my saviour, and I am so thankful for that.

I was born with a desire to win bound up with an innate stubbornness, and this seemed to be the only personality trait that was holding on. My stubbornness was very stubborn. I believed I was strong enough to fight this mental distress alone, and in time I would get over it. Because of this, I never felt it necessary to tell my parents a thing. I knew it was irrational behaviour and I did not want to burden them with something I didn't really understand myself. This silence is one of my biggest regrets in life. I am sure they were aware I was wired differently to the average troublesome teen, but I did an incredible job trying to disguise my worries from them. I became a pro. I was always extremely close to my mother. When my father went overseas, we had to pull together and support each other. I really was a mammy's boy. I always had a very strong relationship with my father even though he spent so much of my early life overseas. I respected him immensely. Although he was army-man strict, he was massively open-minded and liberal and always passionately promoted any interest or hobby I presented him with. I had great parents growing up. But this stubbornness that nurtured my silence stopped me seeking help when I needed it most.

One day, a few months before my Junior Cert, I sat in my room in a dangerously low state. The pressure of exams and my ongoing struggle with anxiety and insomnia combined to create a nasty cocktail of frenzied panic. I'd had enough of this madness that was propelling through my head, thoughts crashing into each other at a million miles an hour. I needed someone to tell me I was going to be okay, that they knew what I was going through. I needed answers, I needed help, yet I was too afraid to ask for it. It occurred to me that the only way to get help was to go to hospital and there, someone could tell me what was wrong with me. And to go to hospital, I had to be sick.

I swallowed a handful of painkillers. Feeling completely calm, I grabbed the chair beside my bed to anchor my arm. I then proceeded to smash my other forearm against the base of the bed with every ounce of strength I had in my body. As I made the initial contact, I felt a sharp pain dart up into my shoulder. It is painful for me to admit now that it felt amazing. It felt euphoric. That is the false and fleeting relief associated with self-harm. I continued to strike my arm with aggression until I could feel the bone just below my elbow move. The outrageous pain that pulsated through my body made me feel alive, and that sense of relief came over me. Relief that I could go into a hospital and tell the doctor what was going on in my head and let them know I did this to myself. A more foolish kind of help-seeking behaviour there couldn't be.

It was clear that I had broken a bone in my arm. The swelling was immediate and the skin had changed colour to a dark shade of blue. I fell back on the bed and lay there in a contemplative dream state. The relief outweighed the considerable pain, and that night, bizarrely, I slept a deep sleep, better than I had in months.

The next day I crept out before anyone in the house had woken, and walked into school cradling a throbbing arm. I told our vice-principal, an understanding fellow, that I had fallen while walking backwards and that my arm had got caught behind me. Having accepted this elaborate lie, he drove me to the hospital where I was X-rayed and told I had a fracture just below my elbow. I was put in plaster and given some powerful painkillers to mask the agony I was experiencing. I was like, fuck, I did a good job. I'd like to do that again, I thought. Needless to say, I really wasn't in a good place.

As the doctor left the treatment room I realised I hadn't said what I was there to say. I had to tell the doctors about the other pain, the one I couldn't quite as easily describe, but which was so much harder to live with, so they could offer a cure. I decided I was going to tell the doctors what had really happened. I built myself up to the point of shaking. I knew my mental anguish was something serious, that it was an illness, though revealing this had more dreadful implications than staying silent. In the Mullingar of my mind, if you had a mental illness, you were sent to an institution. There was only one in the town, a horrible old haunted-looking building called St Loman's. People used to joke about who would end up with 'the crazy nutters'. I didn't realise that as well as going to a hospital there was medication you could take, or therapy you could access. To this day, I recall the quaking dread as I sat in that hospital room in my new cast and waited for the doctor to return. I can't remember clearly what I said, or if I sold it for all it was worth but in a roundabout way I informed the doctor that I had harmed myself. I was fighting back the tears and could barely believe the words that were coming out of my mouth.

This doctor then began to tell me that as teenagers we experience changes and often can feel low or angry. He told me not to worry too much, said that it would pass. Essentially, he was informing me that puberty was the reason I could not sleep at night and the reason I choked for breath and tore my bed sheets apart in terror. Puberty was the reason I broke my own arm off the side of a bed.

I believe that was the lowest point in my life. I left the hospital in a confused and frightened state where the pain I was experiencing mentally far outweighed the physical pain of my fractured limb. The vice-principal drove me home, none the wiser about how I had really broken my arm. Neither were my parents informed of anything amiss. To all the world, I had hurt myself while joking around, but there was nothing funny about how it had happened. Later that evening, my thoughts went dark. That glimpse of hope I had experienced when I made it to the hospital was now overshadowed by crippling fear. Where would I end up? What would they do with me? What would I do to myself?

3. Hard times

I WAS COMPLETELY EMOTIONALLY NUMB, the months after fracturing my arm. In a way, I came to accept this dark and disguised part of my life. I continued to experience panic attacks, almost on a daily basis now. Some not so severe, just a discomfort with being in my own skin, but some that left my mouth clamped and throat spluttering for breath. When I wasn't hyper-tense with fear I found myself becoming aggressive and angry for no apparent reason, which was completely out of character for me. I had little time for my parents and started to alienate myself from my mother. Up until now I had always been fairly honest and open with my mum. She was the most important person in my life, but during this time, I pushed her away. 'You were always a worrier,' she used to tell me, inviting me in her subtle and caring way to reach out to her, but I refused to.

My mother's potential support and empathy was outweighed by the fear and the stigma I imposed on myself. I did not want her to have to deal with the distress of having a son who was self-harming and dealing with serious anxiety issues. Not that I had the language then to even articulate to myself, never mind others, what it was I was dealing with.

When I had room to reflect on what was happening, I felt stupid and embarrassed that I lived with this. I would watch the news in the evening and witness people dealing with famine, war and poverty, and curse myself for being so weak and pathetic. What do I have to be worried about, I'd wonder. Think of the starving kids in Africa. Think of the terrified children in Bosnia as genocide and war crimes destroy their families and country. I would emotionally beat myself to a pulp when I threw perspective into the equation, which is why today, I sincerely encourage loved ones or friends not to use the 'Snap out of it' or 'Sure what have you got to be worried about?' lines when approaching people they think are experiencing mental distress.

At age 15, the warm, everyday conversations I used to have with my mother became strained and awkward, and eventually receded into the past. This brought a new anomaly into my relationship with my head. Guilt.

Guilt robbed me of my self-esteem. I despised myself. Looking back, I feel one of the core and fundamental reasons I refused to seek help was because I felt like I was just a spoilt brat. Here I was, living in a lovely home on the outskirts of Mullingar, with an amazing family, going to a good school, while other teenagers my age were starving to death or being bombed in their beds while sleeping. I took this guilt out on others. I wanted to have a shit life, so at least I could attribute some cause to why I was struggling mentally. Maybe if my parents broke up, or I got an incurable disease, I could dilute some of this guilt, I thought to myself. I would have an alibi for the pain I couldn't explain to myself.

As the guilt progressed, allied with the frustration and fear of anxiety attacks, I encountered a new experience in my life. I would get low. But this was nothing like before; now, I felt so low that I could not get out of my bed on days I didn't have to, and every ounce of motivation or drive was drained from my body. I lacked any empathy and felt emotionally extinct. Things that used to bring me touches of comfort or happiness now offered nothing. I would invent elaborate illnesses, playing them out to perfection so I wouldn't have to face school or what seemed like pointless conversations with friends and even family. In a strange way, making up physical illnesses offered me a break from the constant worry of panic attacks, and once I had a reason to be low, I simply didn't care enough to panic.

The timing of all this was far from ideal. Leading up to my Junior Cert exams, I was observing the constant obsession of my peers and classmates to prove their academic worth, as human development was largely ignored in our schools. We read *One Flew Over the Cuckoo's Nest*, Shakespeare's tragedies and Milton's *Paradise Lost*, without any understanding of what mental illness is, though it stood behind core themes in these texts. I feel now that these were missed chances to educate us subtly on what emotional distress and wellbeing are. I probably wouldn't have been a champion English student, but here was a 15-year-old boy carrying a silent and heavy burden which might have been lifted somewhat by literature. Instead, I remember being told by my teachers how important these exams were in building towards the Leaving Cert. These exams meant nothing to me. Motivation to learn off Irish poems and decipher quadratic equations was relatively low as I sought a way to cope with my anxiety and dangerously low moods.

That way, I found, was to exercise to exhaustion, to eliminate through hours of sport any time to think. I was playing Gaelic with the senior team in my school, one of the younger players at 15. When Westmeath won the 1995 Minor All Ireland for the first time, half of the team were in my school, and I felt a little bit inspired by those lads. They were such heroes, when they walked around people held them in high regard, even the teachers held them in reverence. I thought, I'd love that, I'd love to be a hero. If I got an All Ireland medal, things would be all good. When anxiety racked me, a tough session of Gaelic or rugby cooled me off and that evening I would sleep blissfully. But even sport couldn't suppress the deep unease in me, and anxious thoughts that lay dormant would waken once I was alone.

The Junior Cert came around, and I watched my classmates suffer with stress and anxiety before each exam. Some declaring how little study they had done for this subject and how they hoped a certain question would come up. Others would declare how they could not sleep and felt sick with fear, and how they couldn't wait until it was all over, as I thought to myself, fuck you. Try live with this 24/7. I breezed through my Junior Cert, not because I was well prepared or smart, but because I could not care less. I was so numb to anxiety and stress that it just felt like any other day. Funnily enough, I did quite well, results-wise. And as we know, in the education system, that's all that matters.

Before Third Year ended, the school delivered some news that dealt a blow to the fragile shell of my small world. We were informed that they were ceasing teaching music as a subject for the Leaving Cert. I was raging. It was the only subject that brought me a glimmer of happiness. I wouldn't say music gave me hope, but it made me less pessimistic about the future and academically, I wanted to learn as much as possible. Music, before, had meant a cool instrument I strummed in my room. Now I realised music was an art. I was opening my senses to every genre, the classical pieces that filled the house from my mother's violin, the blues and jazz my brother would play on the piano, a shelf full of old jazz records I was making my way through after school, while also discovering The Beatles, The Beach Boys, The Rolling Stones. Later, when I found out that The Beach Boys' Brian Wilson went through severe anxiety and depression, I couldn't believe a man who wrote such uplifting melodies was going through such distress. I would watch my brother play our piano at home and promise myself that one day I would play as well as him. My mother was a music teacher and our love of music was always a good source of conversation.

She used to teach beginners' violin in our house. I am not sure how many of you have heard a novice violin player screech through 'Mary Had a Little Lamb' on a loop, but I now often joke to my mum that as a teenager, this constant audio assault was the reason for my condition.

Just like when I played sports, playing music, I forgot myself. I needed to continue studying music through my Leaving Cert, but it was clear it would not be in St Mary's CBS, in Mullingar. This left me with no option but to move school. Quite a huge decision for any teenager to make, but for me it was made easier by the fact that I was so isolated from my classmates and peers that I really wasn't leaving anything behind. Plus, I felt that a change or new direction in my life might lead to my issues disappearing. A common belief I practised into the future, the belief that the next new thing you do will rid you of your demons. Slowly, I learned through experience that these demons come with you and haunt you regardless of what you are doing, or where you are going. Ultimately, you will one day have to face them and stop running away.

I decided to attend a boarding school in my town as a day pupil, in order to continue my studies in music. St Finian's offered a music scholarship programme for the Leaving Cert called the Schola, and I was lucky enough to be accepted onto the programme after a fairly rigid interview process. I was to be one of just 14 other boys in the music class. Teenage me figured that this intense focus on one particular subject that I love might help distract me from my hostile mind. For the first time in years I felt a sense of excitement. I had always sung in choirs, and during the summer leading up to the new semester in my new school, I stayed glued to my guitar and piano and spent long afternoons brushing up on my mum's musical theory books.

I wanted to claw back some of the identity I had lost over the years of silence. I grew my hair down to my shoulders and then decided to embrace the mid-nineties' undercut style phenomenon. I also decided to bleach my hair, which turned out to be a nice urine blonde. I looked like a poor man's Hanson tribute act, but the fact that I cared enough to do it was progress enough. I did up my older brother's racer so I could cycle into school in the mornings. It was a fair distance from home so I wasn't going to walk. I had to cycle past Loreto, the girls' school on the way to St Finian's. As reclusive as I was when it came to friends, I was a Tibetan monk when it came to women. I was petrified of them, so I used to tear past Loreto on my bike at an impressive speed so as to go unnoticed. I was six-foot odd, had a head of hair on me like a failed wrestler and a bike that squeaked uncontrollably anytime I pedalled over 5km an hour. I am pretty sure they saw me, and dread to think what they made of me.

In September of Fifth Year, as I cycled up the long driveway to my new school, I prayed it would be the beginning of something better. St Finian's certainly at that time had a different atmosphere to my old school. It was the more academically focused school of our town, with stricter teachers and a more target-based, austere learning environment. It was a very well respected boarding school. As a day pupil who could escape home after the bell rang, I didn't understand how other boys could actually live there, it troubled me. The idea of students having to sleep, eat and essentially live where they went to school seemed inhuman. Jesus, if I had to live there on top of everything else, I reckon education would have been an impossibility. The smell of the processed budget dinners being cooked in the school canteen made me very thankful that I could go home to a decent meal that wasn't turfed out on a tray. That and a lunchtime snack of penny sweets and crisps in Mrs B's shop – which was basically the sitting room of a house next to the school – sustained my teenage diet.

It was evident I was an outsider when I walked into the school, an idea I was relatively comfortable with. No one had any opinions of me, or knew anything about me, apart from the fact that I was rocking the worst hairstyle the corridors of St Finian's had ever witnessed. Most of the students had gone through the previous three years together so were well aware of each other but I was an unknown entity. I decided I would try to sculpt an identity for myself. I signed up for all the school sports teams and even started playing music with some guys after class had finished. I'd pick a Beatles song like 'Lucy in the Sky with Diamonds' and we'd sit around the school desks and play and harmonise. For the first few weeks, my new school served as a kind of release that had been missing from my life. I made a few friends and I was finding myself focusing more on my academic ambitions. To say I felt normal may be over-selling it, but I felt more motivated and purposeful than I had for some time.

About a month into the semester I began to attend evening study classes in school. Five or six hundred pupils from First Year to Leaving Cert would cram into the study hall for three hours a night to vacantly stare at their textbooks, trying to stay awake, as one of the priests would circle the hall, ready to verbally attack anyone not adhering to study-hall etiquette. This environment really was uncomfortable for me, the mass exposure to so many people. I used to scratch the skin on my arm raw, as I prayed that I wouldn't get an anxiety attack in front of all my fellow classmates. I developed a nervous tick whereby I would rub the side of my face aggressively, and I would often take deep breaths to try to keep myself together. The guys around me used to give me this weird look at the moments when I would almost leap out of my seat trying to catch a breath. I was perpetually on the verge of a panic attack, that suffocating anguish that has left a stain on my memory. Instead of leaping from the desk I'd hold onto it, and count down the minutes until the bell went and I could get the hell out of this cauldron of unease.

Even outside of this internal warfare, there wasn't a very nice atmosphere at my new school. Our teachers' vigilance did nothing to stop the large-scale systematic bullying that was going on in the school. It was difficult to watch, especially in the study hall. If an overweight guy got up to use the toilet the entire hall would make a heavy grunting noise, while if a quiet or nervous guy stood up, the hall would make a blowing noise to insinuate that he was homosexual – back then, a justifiable target for cruelty. I would watch these bullied people's faces as they walked down the corridor and notice the seriously distressing effect it was having on them emotionally. I remember one guy, who a few years earlier had soiled himself in class; every time he moved in the hall, 500 people would chant 'shitty arse'. He would shake with nerves as he walked around the school, constantly looking over his shoulder.

Witnessing the mental turmoil these guys were being put through had a devastating effect on me. A lot of my music scholarship class were bearing the brunt of the bullying, the clever, eccentric types who didn't automatically 'fit in'. To my core I detested seeing people like them being picked on. Toxic environments made the panic inside so much worse, and duly, I took on other people's problems. I was a big guy so the bullies never came near me or even tried to cross that bridge, but I was sharing a small class with a group of guys who were getting torn apart on a daily basis, both mentally and physically. I would think, as bad as my problems are, what are these guys going through?

This outlined another shift in my anxiety problems. In general, I did not worry about anyone except for those in my family. I worried about myself and the issues I was facing. However, now I would go home after study and start thinking of the hell these guys were going through in school. Were they getting beaten up in their dorms as I lay here safely in my bed at home? Were they crying themselves to sleep, in fear of what would happen to them the next day? I would be cut down with panic attacks thinking of what was happening to them, even though I did not really know them. I tried to step in a few times and stand up to the bullying, just to give myself some peace of mind when I went home. I remember pinning one of the bullies to a wall and nearly choking him and head-butting him in the process. Once again, totally out of character for me. I was arched with frustration at what was happening to that lad, and my powerlessness to prevent it. I realised that I had to start to control this aggression and anger, otherwise I would do something stupid.

I threw myself into sport. I must have played for every sports team in the school: Gaelic, hurling, soccer, golf and athletics. I had really grown into my body and was starting to recognise that I had ability across all sports. I was relatively quick for my height and had a lot of built-in aggression that I needed to get out of me. In Israel I had grown to love sport, in my previous school I had recognised the positive benefits of physical activity, but at St Finian's I found myself exploring it in a far more profound way.

I would miss hours of school and study as I had to travel to play Gaelic matches all over Leinster and beyond. I slowly began to integrate with my team-mates and saw the importance of this positive interaction with my peers as we aimed at a common goal. I found that when I was training or playing matches I was so focused on the particular task in hand that I literally did not have time to let my rogue thoughts run riot in my head. My teachers or parents could not figure out where I got the energy from. To me, sport served as a crutch, or a type of medication for my mental health problems. It also allowed me to focus my aggression in a more controlled and positive way.

I have rarely in my life been good at sitting still. A restless energy mills around inside me until I have a use for it. At 16, when I wasn't out playing sport, I was making plans for music. I joined a band called Kaja with my music pals, many of them boarders from Trim and Navan. We would jam out old Beatles covers in the music room during study breaks. Music was always my companion. No matter how bad things got, playing the guitar and singing a few tunes always offered me some solace. I owe so much to music and am blessed to have it in my life. That and sport were my sources of support and still are today. They helped me to rebuild my self-esteem and also slowly helped me regain some form of social life.

It is difficult now to recall that behind closed doors, I was still in a perpetual conflict with my mind. The relief that music and sport would bring would be long forgotten when I lay in bed inviting my anxiety to take me over. I would find myself feeling physically sick, while observing the grotesque bullying that was going on, and then I would always bring it home with me. In my more courageous moments I would try to reason with the bullies and explain that they should leave these guys alone, that they had been through enough. It fell on deaf ears. The bullying was structural and filtered down through each year. The sixth years would bully the fifth years and fifth years would bully third years and so on. It became unbearable to watch. Some days, I would simply get up during class and leave for home, perhaps stopping in Mrs B's for some sweets to fuel my cycle and get there as quickly as possible.

I started mitching from school or faking illness so I didn't have to attend. But then I could not play sport, or jam with my mates. I was stuck in a fucked-up place and at times I just wanted to go into my school with a bat and slap the heads off all the bullies. In a weird way, they were indirectly bullying me too. I felt that the teachers knew what was happening but could do little to prevent it. It's almost as if this was just part of growing up for some kids. Not only were we not being taught about mental health or given coping strategies, some kids had to be mentally and physically tortured by their classmates as well. Bullying has lifelong consequences for those affected by it. It's a deeply complex issue. Those doing the bullying are often doing it as a result of issues at home or elsewhere, so severely reprimanding the bully is not going to solve the problem. I hate to think of what it's like for kids now, facing the added pressure of negotiating social media.

After six months, I decided that I was not able to stay in this school. I told my mother that I wanted to repeat the year as at this stage I had missed so much class I had fallen far behind. Word had got back to my old school, St

Mary's, that I had developed into a talented midfielder on the football team and on account of this, they offered me a place to repeat fifth year, which I immediately accepted. I needed to get out of the environment I was in, even if it meant sacrificing music as a Leaving Cert subject. As luck would have it, a few of my childhood friends had decided they wanted to repeat fifth year, including my future band mate, The Blizzards' drummer Dec Murphy. This helped me with the transition as these guys were top lads. Dead sound and straight up and honest. We developed quite a small and intimate crew of friends, and the bullying I'd become accustomed to seeing at St Finian's wasn't tolerated or accepted by either the teachers or the other guys in the school.

My group of friends and I kept ourselves to ourselves but at this stage, I had become a promising athlete. I was playing midfield for my school's senior team in Gaelic and I was also developing a reputation as a strong rugby player. Having played with my local rugby club, Mullingar, I began breaking into the Leinster youth set-up. Much of this had to do with my size – by now a lanky 6 foot 4 inches – but also because some of the guys in my local area were breaking into the squad as well, making excellent competition. These were the same friends I had isolated myself from over the previous few years, but they unquestioningly welcomed me back and this was incredibly important to me. My mates Butch, Beano, Nicolas and Eoiny were as mad as hens, but the types of guys you wanted in your corner if the shit hit the fan. They may not have seen the importance of their friendship to me, the prodigal son, but this reconnection we made is one of the reasons I was able to become a professional rugby player. I owe those guys so much and over the years, though we're still young, we have gone through an awful lot together.

Although I was achieving as an athlete, I still felt like a fraud. Here I was, tearing into lads on the rugby pitch and punching dressing room walls before football matches but behind it all I was a fragile young guy, silently struggling with his demons. As my reputation grew as a tough, competitive athlete, I saw it almost as a front to the brittle person within. I felt I had to be fooling everyone. Don't get me wrong, I remember this period of my life with fondness too, but many good memories are shrouded by those early struggles with panic attacks, insomnia and very unstable, dark moods. And with all this, something else was happening. I was beginning to recognise how I could use my struggles to give me an edge over others. I was beginning to recognise that there were things I could do to ease the distress. And most importantly of all, I was beginning to recognise that the environment I was in often had a worsening impact on my mental health. As ever, toxic, negative environments contributed to toxic, negative thoughts, which led to toxic, negative behaviours.

4. Bet-down and bald

FOR MANY, COLLEGE IS THE turning point in life, where self-expression and experimentation are celebrated and nurtured, while identity is fine-tuned and your core values are defined. The vice grip constraints of overly protective parents and a totalitarian education system suddenly lose their grasp, and teenagers become adults, almost overnight. Alcohol and processed foods become the staple diet, while the opposite sex becomes more prominent indeed – especially coming from an all-boys' school. This sudden deviation from the normality of teenage years is a change the vast majority of our youth are not fully prepared for, on many different fronts, but none more so than in the mental and emotional maturity required for their new lives.

I was blessed to be offered a rugby scholarship to University College Dublin. It was not only a huge plus for my development as a rugby player, but also took a slight financial burden off my parents who had already put three of my siblings through full-time third-level education. Although I rather ambitiously had Physiotherapy down on my CAO form as my course of choice for third level, I had not worked hard enough for my Leaving Cert to achieve the points needed, so I found myself studying for a Bachelor of Arts degree in Economics, Sociology and Psychology. It was an interesting and eclectic mix of subjects that put quite a stamp on my future endeavours, although I can barely spell those words now.

I was pleased the day I packed up my belongings for my mother to drive me to UCD, where I was to live with three people I had never met. I felt this new and exciting chapter in my life would definitely mask my issues and, in time, make them go away. On the journey to Dublin, I convinced myself that my crippling anxiety and depressive episodes were a result of location and environment rather than something more sinister. This is a common trend that has shadowed my relationship with my mental health. My thought processes would be humorous if they weren't so tragically flawed. If it were a physical issue such as a broken leg or, say, some disease, would it go away if you went somewhere else? In most cases, of course not, so the fact I believed I could outrun a mental illness was deeply naive and no doubt a side effect of the lack of information and education on the subject in such a stigmatised society as Ireland.

My mother's car pulled into the stony surrounds of UCD the day before college began. As a scholarship student, I was offered on-site campus accommodation that was fully paid for. The apartments were identical blocks of sandstone red, a cross between a three-star holiday resort and a Russian communist camp. Inside they were cold and sterile. When my mum hugged me goodbye and I had piled everything into the house, I decided to scope the place out a bit. I walked down to the student shop to buy some Super Noodles, the nutrition choice of most college students. As I made my way there, every single apartment in our block seemed to be playing David Gray's *White Ladder*. So many 18-year-old girls prostrating their emotions to those melancholy tunes. I was thinking lads, please, as if living with depression isn't hard enough, I now have to listen to 'Babylon' 40 times a day.

On my first day of college, taking the short walk through campus to the faculty, I sensed an uneasiness that I often experienced when facing an unknown situation. I walked cautiously down the main strip of UCD towards the arts block, which aesthetically would not have looked out of place in a Second World War movie. It seemed that whoever was responsible for the building was allergic to the notion of a lick of paint, but at least it was easy to spot. When I stopped an older student to ask the way there, I was just told to look out for the dullest, ugliest building I could see.

As I approached the side entrance of the building, I could feel the tightness begin to take hold in my chest.

When I opened the door, an explosion of zealous Fresher students erupted from one of the lecture theatres as if they had just been issued a bomb threat. It was a manic scene that immediately resulted in my losing all composure. I did not realise that that amount of make-up actually existed; it was as if the Brown Thomas department store just hologrammed in front of me. I didn't even have a chance to react and before I knew it I was gasping for air, almost suffocating in front of all my new college mates. Utilising my now 17 stone, 6 foot 6 inch frame I put my rugby experience to good use, as I literally barraged the congregation out of my way. It was like Moses parting the Red Sea. Next I frantically looked for the safety of the toilets. It was less like a heroic biblical scene when I locked myself into a toilet cubicle and stayed there palpitating for almost four hours. The best part of the day was dispensed of hunched on the floor, wrestling one vicious anxiety attack. I was truly frazzled, but quite calculated in my approach to secrecy at the same time. In my head there was no way I was going near the arts block again until the gang of Freshers had made their way to the student bar.

I mapped out the best way back to campus where I wouldn't need to be exposed to such mass crowds, and once the din had died away, I sheepishly opened the toilet door and navigated my way back to the tiny room in my flat, where I sat zonked on the bed, wondering to myself how the fuck was I going to get through college and maintain my scholarship if I couldn't even face a lecture without hibernating in the UCD arts block toilets for hours on end.

The following morning I took two 5mg Xanax tablets. It was remarkably easy to get my hands on black-market prescription meds during my time in college, and I am uncomfortable remembering my tendency for self-medication, scoring Xanax and Valium the way other people scored hash. But, liking the effects of these drugs, I always tried to keep a few in my wallet as a kind of crutch. I waited an hour until I felt that artificial calm that benzodiazepines offer kick through, and then floated down to college, barely paying attention to the thousands of people who were wandering too, cluelessly looking for their lecture theatre. I walked into my class confidently, perhaps with the relaxed air of The Fonz from the 1980s sitcom *Happy Days*, a marked contrast from the nervous wreck of the previous afternoon. I really didn't know if I was in the right hall but thanks to the magic of modern medicine, I really didn't care. I could see the lecturer's mouth moving but I had no idea what was coming out. My head felt heavy and I just wanted to put my arms on the desk and have a mid-lecture snooze, when suddenly I heard this almighty thud, only to see a modestly sized perished salmon lying inches from my face.

Now, I had heard horror stories regarding the abuse of prescription medication before, and I had taken Xanax on quite a few occasions, but I had never seen or heard of a flying salmon. The entire hall screamed in comedic shock as my senses were still very much in slow-motion mode, reacting as if I were rather used to the idea of an airborne dead fish. As I became more aware of the situation I realised the fish was thrown into the lecture hall by some lads who had overindulged in the happy hour deals from the student bar and were doing it as some kind of dare. In my stoned state I laughed off the incident, but thinking back, if it had happened the previous day I am pretty sure I would have been down in St Vincent's Hospital on the defibrillator.

There is a phase of first year college that swam by in a merry haze of Valium. The drug gave me a vicious hangover. My upper and lower mouth would be stuck together like glue and my head would pound, and I would wake up with the fear of a thousand hangovers put together. But it was a minor issue; this pill took my sickening anxiety away. All I wanted was a break, just for a few hours, and Valium provided a prolonged release. It's for this reason that drugs such as these are so dangerously addictive. You feel you need to take more to offset the hangover from the Valium the day before and hence the vicious circle continues. Thankfully, some sense prevailed in the back of my mind. I was petrified of the drug, knowing its addictive nature, and also knew I would never hold down a rugby scholarship if I was consuming copious amounts of benzodiazepines.

It was clear this was not sustainable behaviour. The idea of taking a handful of Valium every time I set foot in college was not something I was prepared to do, and I am glad I had enough awareness of the drug to know the damage it can do if abused. Although I was not prepared to self-medicate in order to attend college, I was equally unprepared to face the lectures. As I was on a sports scholarship, I felt I could not be that person who has panic attacks or suffers with anxiety. We were the jocks, the tough guys, not the guys who lock themselves in toilets or go home with their eyes pinned to the ground. My logic was invincible, I figured. Jesus, thinking back, I was a mess.

At that time, I couldn't conceive of the idea that anyone else could be going through similar issues to me. I took those I encountered, in sports and beyond, at face value – as they may well have taken me, oblivious to what was going on beneath the surface of my personality. Had I realised then what I know now, I would have felt a lot less isolated. Appearances, you come to learn, are all well and good, but they don't tell even a fraction of a person's story.

At UCD, I felt this irrational paranoia that if I went to a counselling service in the college or visited the chaplain, somehow this would get back to my coaches and managers in the rugby club and they would judge me and label me as weak. I realise now how devoid of logic it is but when you experience generalised anxiety disorder – the term I came to know my condition by – the ability to think logically is lost on you and you become a professional at thinking the worst. It's a situation many people who suffer from anxiety find themselves in on a daily basis, locked into a needless dilemma about informing their bosses or peers that they deal with mental distress and worrying that they will lose their jobs or be mocked. Dealing with anxiety, depression and other mental health concerns is incredibly testing and difficult without the added fear of being stigmatised by the draconian attitude that is deeply ingrained in a culture where the admission that we are not all emotionally invincible is frowned upon.

As spring of my first year turned to summer, rugby held me in one piece, but I found I couldn't attend lectures. The year was nearly over and I had learned precious little about Economics, Sociology and Psychology. As a result, I was faced with no option but to defer my first year exams until the following year. I thought about dropping out of college but I was not prepared to lose my rugby scholarship. The focus of training and playing matches really was the only thing that brought me comfort at this time. I would have struggled for survival without its welcome distraction; that, and my guitar. I was able to channel my frustrations and anger on the pitch and it was an incredible release. I trained and played with the same intensity and really enjoyed the cohesion of a team environment even though I felt like I was cheating on my team-mates. When my insomnia returned I would just train harder so when I came home in the evening my body had no choice but to give up and let me sleep; when my anxiety attacks resurfaced I would spend hours in the gym lifting weights and getting rid of my unwanted adrenaline.

I was also starting to figure out the machinations of my mind, and was able to manage the rough days by submerging myself in training. As effective as this was though, it wasn't sustainable. With each passing day, my physical and mental health were growing further apart. I was putting too much pressure and stress on my body physically, in order to offset the mental problems I was enduring. When my immune system was down, I would quite often get injured and when the result put me out of action, I would become so depressed that I would not be able to eat, sleep or function 'like a normal person' – it was a phrase I adopted when imagining what others were like, 'normal', though we know there isn't a 'normal'. I would spend days in my bed refusing to communicate with anyone, including my physiotherapist and team doctors. At this point sports were almost like an addiction. Training and playing were a potent medication and when I got injured I had to go cold turkey – which was hell-on-earth stuff. Today, in elite sport, an injured player rehabilitates within their squad, for social support. In that day, when you got injured, you were a forgotten soul.

When I played rugby, all the emphasis was on the skill and physical ability of the athlete, while the human aspects were ignored. A player's mother could be dying of cancer and no one in the squad would know, and if that player had an off game or was missing training, they would be labelled lazy or not dedicated. Nowadays, elite teams and coaches are recognising the importance of human development and you would do well to find a top team who has not hired a sports and performance psychologist. But this was a different time. The comparisons with the education system must be made: academic and sporting worth both came before human development.

Regardless of my occasional injuries, I was still very much progressing through the ranks of my sport. As a back row flanker – for my size I was quite fast – I had represented the Leinster Under-21s in the inter-provincials, which we won, and also had my initial trials with the Irish Under-21s set-up. I had another season to go before I could play on the 21s so I didn't put too much pressure on myself to make the squad, but I wanted to make sure the coaches did not forget me. I was also accepted into the Irish Academy, which was a group of elite under-age players, being prepared and guided towards the professional aspects of rugby. My director of rugby in UCD, John McClean, taught me so much about the sport, and I was relatively close to him. He was almost timid, I was angry and aggressive, and between those extremes we connected and held each other in respect. On the surface, he could see a raw talented guy turn into a representative rugby player but, as always, I tried hard to hide the mental cracks that lay under the surface.

In UCD rugby, we were a close-knit bunch of guys who really looked out for each other, even though we had all attended different schools which would have been intense competitors and rivals in the past. I was in the UCD Under-20s squad but was often called into the senior squad for training and back-up. These guys were a bit older and acted like big brothers to me, advising and watching my back in games. Post-match routine always involved alcohol and socialising. After away matches a well-wisher would carry slabs of beer into the dressing rooms, and 24 cans of Heineken would be put away only for the stocks to be replenished for the bus back to Dublin – where after copious Guinness in the pub we'd hit a nightclub, and the dreaded shots.

At that time I would have drunk anything put in front of me. It was the fastest way to bond with the team and besides, our elder supporters – plenty of big shot solicitors with a lot of money in the club – would often put a kitty behind the bar, so we could drink for free all night. Those nights were hardcore, and I would never take a back step when it came to drinking. I had to prove myself to my team-mates, I felt. This drinking culture is massively prevalent in most team sports, seen as an effective way to build team cohesion, but for me it was disastrous. It left me in all sorts of trouble for the week ahead. I have always had a very interesting and unsteady relationship with alcohol. Just like prescription medication, when I consumed alcohol I felt relaxed and dare I say it, happy. It would offer me a sense of normality, and when I felt this wear off, I would drink more, but I couldn't become so intoxicated that I was unable to control my actions. I am a big guy so I can never let myself get to the point of not being able to walk. No one is capable of carrying me anyway. Out drinking, I always made it home.

However, the next day I would become dangerously low. Some people associate hangovers with headaches and nausea; I associate hangovers with acute depression and anxiety. I would have to fight for every last breath throughout the day, which would never be spent with the conventional takeaway and bad movie. I had to get out of the house and keep moving, thinking up anything to occupy my brain and sweat away the tension. Sometimes I found myself walking along the dual carriageway from UCD into the city, where I would wander around in a blank state. I even used to go to the library so as not to be alone with my thoughts. My motivation levels would all but disappear and every time I closed my eyes to sleep, I would encounter the start of a panic attack. Every one of us knows what it's like to have The Fear – that euphemism for depression and anxiety drinking concocts. I had The Fear on a regular basis, and now drinking was adding fuel to the fire. It was never worth it, and that's putting it mildly.

The only thing that would soothe the pain would be to

drink again, or take a Xanax or a Valium or even, a new discovery, a sleeping pill – the last of which again left me bollixed for another few days. People who endure issues with their mental health really need to ask themselves tough questions about alcohol. Regardless of its open availability and its ingrained place in our culture, it's still a drug and if abused can be unquantifiably dangerous.

These attacks became a terrible prospect, enough to deter a loose cannon rugby player from his beloved drinking sessions. I would make up incredible lies to get out of going on the piss with the squad sometimes. I would tell them I had to go home to help my dad on the farm. My dad is in the army, for God's sake, but Dublin folk tend to believe if you live down the country you own a farm, so they never questioned me on it. When I ended up on the beer, I was a bottomless pit, I could drink and drink and drink where pints were concerned. I did try my best to avoid the trays of sickening shots that were thrown my way, but more often than not I would get very drunk and suffer the consequences.

In Ireland, we often refuse to believe that alcohol, if abused, can be as damaging as a drug. But it's not like you have to look hard to see its devastation. Families and communities are torn apart by alcohol abuse, across every demographic, class and gender. Like mental health problems, alcohol addiction crosses all boundaries, yet as a society we still resist accepting its dangers. I am often asked by people dealing with anxiety and depression what they can do to help themselves. I am cautious about offering direct advice as I am not qualified to do so, but one thing I always address is alcohol, society's drug of choice. It's important to establish what your unique personal relationship with alcohol is, as it affects everyone differently. If you are going out on the weekends and getting destroyed and then spending the rest of the week in mental distress, or abusing more alcohol or prescription meds to get some sleep, you have to ask yourself, honestly, is it worth it? It was certainly a question I avoided posing to myself. Drink was part of being a rugby player. We needed to fit in. The youthful energy made me just about able to deal with its ugly effects.

During the summer of 2000, I set some goals both academically and in terms of sport. I knew that if I were to re-engage with the college environment I would have to make some changes. I went home to Mullingar for the summer to train, but I also started reading and practising meditation. I had read a few newspaper articles which said that mindfulness can be effective for a person's mental health, but also for their focus and concentration on their chosen passions. I always struggled with meditation, and still do. As soon as I intentionally start concentrating on my breathing, I tend to hyper-ventilate, which in turn results in panic. However, the more I read about meditation and the benefits of being present in the moment, the more I realised that it wasn't entirely based upon controlled breathing. In one article I found out about the body scanning and visualisation techniques which would become deeply comforting during anxiety attacks and help calm my heart rate and boost my mood. At the time I failed to fully grasp what being present actually meant. It took years to develop that sense of 'now', until it was explained to me in a very simple phrase by a close friend, Marty Mulligan. He told me once that people who are depressed are always thinking of the past, people who have anxiety are always thinking of the future, people who are happy are always thinking of now.

These alternative therapies marked my first attempts at looking at ways to pro-actively manage and deal with my issues. A few years late, but it wasn't *too* late. I went back to college that September a much stronger athlete, finally recognising my own potential. I had spent three months training to be physically strong, but crucially, I was starting to look at ways to control my anxiety and depressive episodes. I still wasn't prepared to seek professional help, cowering from the ridiculous stigma that may have awaited. I could not present weakness. I was the sports scholarship representative, tough and confident, with the leadership quality a team needed. If you were being paid to be a rugby player, you had to be a pillar of strength, a person people could turn to at all times. To be depressed, to be anxious, meant being a quiet, weakened person in the corner, according to the stereotype. I couldn't give in to that possibility, and aware that I had a problem, any signs of progress made me feel like I could cope on my own.

Walking back into the arts block for the first day of lectures, I was more prepared for the onslaught but I still was incredibly uneasy in this environment. Sitting in my first lecture was a daunting experience. Five hundred students pretending they cared about the socialist economic theories of Karl Marx, while I prayed that a fish would not be pelted into the theatre in my direction. It was an absurd set-up. This was one of the first situations where I began to put visualisation techniques into practice, to survive the alienation I felt. I would try to visualise myself playing a match or performing a certain task within the match, which removed me, mentally, from this environment of uneasiness. It certainly had a positive effect. However, it also had its side-effects: I learned nothing in class.

A month or two back at college, I was introduced to a girl after one of our club matches with UCD. Always guarded, it was close to impossible for me to let anyone into my world. My daily struggles were a well-kept secret, and if I allowed a girl that I liked to get close, she could find out. Jesus Christ, she might think, he's a freak. And what if I had a panic attack? If I had a panic attack, she could tell her mates, they could tell their boyfriends, and those lads might have played rugby with me. They'd think: he is fucking crazy. College was a closely bound network. If you kissed somebody on the weekend, everybody found out. If you lost it, everybody would get wind of that too. But you were a rugby player: you had to have a pretty girlfriend to complete the picture. In our idiocy, we even permitted the shorthand 'rugger huggers', for aspiring girlfriends of rugby players. Of course, part of me craved to be understood, to connect with somebody, and here was this girl, who seemed interesting, in a bar after one of our matches. We swapped numbers. That week we went out for a few drinks and it developed from there.

It was fraught from the get-go. I would generally ignore her calls, spending the majority of my time in college trying to avoid her. It was ridiculous and incredibly juvenile. She thought I was just being a typical jock, playing her, but the reality was, I was terrified of her finding out about what was going on beneath the surface. She would want to come over to my place on campus and I just could not let it happen. I feared I would not be able to hide the way I was. The talk would begin: she would tell her mates, they would tell their boyfriends, they would tell my team-mates, and they would tell my coaches. It was an awkward situation, to say the least. She was a lovely person who did not deserve to be messed around. It was like a fucked-up *Dawson's Creek* episode. Where those characters indulged their emotions in daily psychobabble, I fenced mine in until the situation became fraught with tension.

One sweltering hot May day coming up to exams, my girlfriend stormed into the library while I was attempting to study and tore the head off me in front of a group of very entertained students. I remember her calling me a bald, bet-down bollix. An interesting, fairly accurate portrayal of my jock persona, which included a shaven head at that time. I was always a fan of alliteration, so behind my obvious mortification, I was impressed. She threw her phone at me, shouting that she said she'd been trying to contact me, and demanding to know why I hadn't replied to her messages. Sitting there, stunned and red-faced at my desk, I was speechless. That's when the relationship came to its natural conclusion.

Although my love life was, at best, non-existent, the dedication I put into training during the summer months was really beginning to pay dividends, and soon I was drafted into the Irish Under-21s squad, after a successful run with the Leinster Under-21s. Initially it was just a training squad, but I was somewhat confident that I had the ability to make the team and was widely tipped to be the blind-side flanker for the upcoming match against a select under-20s New Zealand touring team.

They were to announce the squad a few weeks before the match. I felt I had done more than enough to earn my place there so when I received a letter from the IRFU to tell me I had unfortunately not made the 24-man squad I was devastated. Lying on my bed, reading the lines of their rejection over and over, I felt a numbness settle in. What was I going to tell my dad? My mother didn't come to my matches, being too afraid of seeing me get hurt, but my dad was an avid supporter, and so proud. What would he think of me? What would John McClean think? Furthermore, what had I done wrong? I was well ahead of the guy who took my place, I'd thought.

That night, I was inconsolable. I went into my tiny room and just lay on the bed, thinking. I really struggled to know if it was worth it all. Rugby at this level was about climbing further up the ranks and if you didn't reach that goal your life was ripped apart, in our none-too-mature understanding of things. Sport is all about highs and lows, and the ability to cope with failure is paramount to becoming a successful athlete, but for me sport meant something else. It was the only thing that helped clear the mess that was in my mind.

The sickness of my mood infiltrated my body, as it always does, and I vomited uncontrollably all night, retching until there was nothing in my stomach. I had no appetite and I could not face food. The next morning I stayed in my bed with the blinds pulled down and stared at one spot on the ceiling for hours. A crack in the bland, sterile box that was my room. I was flatlined. Emotionally, at that point, nothing other than being in that squad mattered. Not family, not friends, not the joy of playing sport. That's the thing about depression that really destroyed me. I love my family more than anything on this planet, yet when I experienced these lows, family became irrelevant. I became more and more isolated. The guilt compounded the pain. When you ignore your mother as she calls to see if you're okay, when you know she is at home worried to death, but you pretend you can't answer, you start to wonder, what kind of horrible human being am I? A self-loathing consumes you. You believe you cannot face being in your own skin. Madness replaces rationale as you start to pull your hair out with frustration. You cannot catch your breath as you sob aimlessly. It's not like you are feeling sorry for yourself and want attention, the last thing you want is attention. You want the world and everything in it to disappear. You want to remain in the darkness so no one can find you.

I went through this compulsive horror for three days, wondering if I would ever get out of it. In the back of my head, I knew from experience I would recover, just like you do from a bout of flu. Hard as hell for a few days but then your immune system rebuilds itself and you start feeling human again. It is the same with my depressive episodes. I know they will pass and it's this realisation that gets me through every time. I have a resentment for the careless use of the phrase 'positive mental health'. When you are acutely struggling it's virtually impossible to remain positive. In my case, to have positive mental health is to believe that regardless of how dark it is, regardless of how hopeless you feel, it will always pass. Those days, that belief eluded me.

Sleep deprivation really did not help the situation. So when I managed to eke out just four or five hours of kip after three days of hell, I started experiencing glimpses of normality. I was hungry, I wanted to watch television, I wanted to talk to someone.

The afternoon that I emerged, several days later, my phone flashed with a number I didn't recognise so I let it ring out. A message pinged. I cautiously had a listen and was surprised to hear the voice of the manager of the Irish Under-21s squad telling me to call him back. I immediately called him and he told me that one of the players in my position had picked up a serious injury in training and I had been drafted into the squad. Having barely slept or eaten in the previous three days my reaction was somewhat muted. We had a training camp that weekend and I wasn't in much of a state either mentally or physically to go through an intense two-day session with the Irish squad. I had to get myself together, so I went to the supermarket and bought a mountain of food to try to regain some lost energy. I chucked it all in: Goodfella's pizzas, Super Noodles, sliced pan, ham, cheese, Haribos, wine gums. The very worst foods to be eating. And I sat there at home, making my way through processed food heaven. I visited the campus doctor to see if I could bluff some sleeping pills so I could at least get a good night's sleep. I told him I had not slept in a week due to 'college pressures', so he gave me two or three pills which did the trick. On one hand, I was relieved I had been brought back into the squad but I was also worried as I knew the previous few days had drained me. I was running on empty but this was my last chance and I knew it, so I dug deep. I was representing my country in a couple of days' time, putting on an Irish jersey. Wearing that jersey before the match, going back on the pitch to sing the national anthem with my team and those crowds of supporters, made for a very proud feeling.

When I arrived at the hotel for the camp, Des Dillon, one of the senior players on the squad, came up to me and told me that I was robbed in the first place and I should have been there from the start. Everyone looked up to Des, he had the most potential of all of us, so his approval gave me an enormous lift. Part of me still doubted my ability but I trained hard over those two days. I threw myself into tackles with zero regard for my safety and brought an intensity that was fuelled by the frustration, disappointment and anger of the previous week. This was patently evident to the selectors. I suppose they wanted to see how I reacted to the disappointment of initially being dropped.

That Sunday evening they were announcing the team for the coming weekend's match against the New Zealand Under-20s touring side. We walked into the meeting room and I could sense the anticipation and nervous energy as the squad eagerly awaited to hear their name read out by the coach, starting at number 15 and counting down. I couldn't even listen to any of the other names but as he got closer to the forwards, my body tightened and I closed my eyes, Number 8 Des Dillon, Number 7 Johnny O'Connor, Number 6 Niall Breslin.

My heart almost stopped. I sat in that room trying to regain my composure, though all I wanted to do was run out and ring my parents and tell them, 'I'm starting on the Irish Under-21s!' It had been one hell of a week, from complete darkness into blinding light. For years, I rarely practised self-compassion, a key component of positive psychology, but walking out of that room I gave myself compassion. I really could not have been prouder of myself, not just for making the team, but for having the strength to rebound from adversity.

I vividly remember the game against New Zealand. We won it easily as they had a weakened second team out. I was part of the back row that day and we absolutely dominated the game. Johnny O'Connor, an open-side flanker, was a seriously aggressive and fierce competitor that I had played with previously in the Irish Under-19s squad and we had a field day. That evening I received my first cap for the Irish Under-21s in the Greystones clubhouse. As I left the bar, a jovial, important-looking chap in a suit offered his congratulations, informing me I was his man of the match. I asked one of the lads who he was and it turned out to be Ken Ging, the Leinster senior manager. They were keeping a close eye on me, though little did I know this at the time.

That game secured my spot on the team for the upcoming
Six Nations and after a strong opening victory against the
Italians in Rome we were feeling confident and excited
about the rest of the championship. In Rome, one of the
most entertaining moments was when we were given
a police escort from our hotel on the Saturday morning
after our match to go watch the senior team play. They
brought us right to the front gates of the stadium and into
the coach area under the stand before they realised that
we were the under-21s and not the senior squad. Dopes.

Next up, the flair of the French in Dublin, which was
always going to be a tough encounter. The Thursday
before the game I came down with a chest infection and
although I tried to train through it, I knew, even in the
warm-up, I was gone. Now this, in fairness, was not
something that upset me too much. I had established
myself on the team and the coach had a lot of faith in
me. We lost that match narrowly and the rest of the
season was cancelled due to the unfortunate foot-and-
mouth epidemic. Our focus turned to the World Cup
in Australia the coming summer. I was gaining self-
confidence, training so hard, and that lovely exhaustion
got the better of my moods, allowing me to sleep at
night. Sleep was the greatest gift I could give myself.

In the months leading up to the World Cup I took good
care of myself. I had to gain weight so I ate well, and
because I couldn't get the calories I needed from processed
foods, I even started preparing fresh vegetables and meat.

Then one night when I was out with the boys from UCD, having won the club league, I found myself downing whiskey with three of the hardest-drinking players in the squad. Props, of course. I got up from the table to get some air but whiskey has this amazing ability to get your legs drunk before your head. My lower body refused to communicate with my brain and I fell down two small steps in the bar on the way to the toilet.

It was an aberration from my usual physical composure while polluted drunk. Straight away I could feel the intense pain shoot up from my ankle. My immediate feeling was I had broken my leg. Out of pure embarrassment I stood up, laughing at myself, and hobbled out of the pub leaving my dignity behind. Our team physio, Frances, had been watching this little episode and knew something serious was up so she followed me out and saw me sitting on the kerb with my hands over my face. She took a look at my ankle and told me it was more than likely a ligament tear, which leaves you out for six to eight weeks, minimum. That was it. I was out of the World Cup and I knew it. We were leaving for Australia in four weeks. Because there was so much alcohol in my system the pain had not set in, and I refused to believe it was serious. But the next day, looking at the state of my leg, I knew I was in trouble.

I came relatively clean with my coaches. I told them I had had a few drinks and torn ankle ligaments. To my surprise they said they believed I could get back in time and that they were happy to allow me recover with the hope of returning to training the week before we left. Although the doctor and physio both warned me this was pushing the boundaries of possibility, I refused to accept their advice and right enough, the week before we departed for Sydney I was back on the pitch, heavily strapped, full of painkillers but ready for action, spurred on by the fear of what missing the World Cup would do to me professionally, and more importantly, mentally.

There was a serious buzz in Australia when we arrived, as the British and Irish Lions had just flown in for their tour. As soon as we dropped our bags and checked into the hotel we had an easy session to loosen out our weary muscles after the long 24-hour flight. Something that had been playing on my mind leading up to the World Cup was the fact I would have to share a room with one of my team-mates. They were all good guys but I was paranoid that my insomnia and panic attacks would really piss off whoever ended up as my room-mate. A panic attack has all the appearance of a physical fit. Trembling, spluttering, tears. That desperate attempt to catch a breath that makes your body shake uncontrollably. It's frightening to witness. Whatever unfortunate I ended up sharing with would think I was dying. How relieved I was then, when purely by alphabetical order one of the soundest guys on the tour, Gary Brown, ended up in my room. He was the joker of the squad and incredibly laid back and decent so it comforted me slightly. Just ever so slightly.

The first night in the hotel we were all so jet-lagged that we weren't making sense by 8pm, and everybody slept straight through the night. A rarity for me, but most welcome. However, the following nights were a disaster. I could not sleep a wink and had to try to disguise the heavy sound of breathlessness as I lay in bed. Luckily, Gary was a reliable sleeper but I remember holding pillows over my mouth so he couldn't hear me choking for air each night. I would lie awake and use the light of my phone to read whatever sports biography I had packed, so as not to waken him. This was exhausting but I was not in a position to approach my coaches and manager to tell them why I was not sleeping. I just ploughed on like I had done many times in the past.

Two nights before our first match, I went to bed feeling incredibly on edge. I could not lie in bed without hyperventilating. As Gary innocently watched a DVD on his laptop, I kept pretending I had to go out onto the balcony to make phone calls. When he turned off the light to go to sleep I could feel my chest getting heavy and I began fighting for air. I grappled for something that had helped in the past: music. I tried to sing a song in my head to distract myself from what was happening but before I got to the chorus I was on the hotel floor gasping for air. I used the laundry bag to breathe in and out of slowly, to try and regain some composure in my breathing, but I was too far gone. I crawled out onto the balcony and lay in the corner with the sliding door shut. Amazingly,

Gary slept through the whole thing as I lay shivering and covered in sweat on our storeys-high balcony for hours after the attack. You had to admire him.

The event exhausted my body. I woke up with my cheek on the balcony at 6am to see Gary still snoring, and quietly made my way back into the room and put on my tracksuit to head down for breakfast, pretending all was grand. Was it fuck. The breakfast felt like acid as it hit my stomach and I knew I wasn't going to keep it down. I was also paranoid Gary had heard what had happened and was telling the lads that I had a freak-out or something. I was amazed when he came down to breakfast without a bother on him; luckily he had been sound asleep in dreamland while I was in my nightmare.

You see, the issue with anxiety is not just having the panic attacks, it's living with the constant dread that they could come at any time. I kept thinking we could be in a team meeting and I would feel one come on and have a full-blown attack in front of everyone. It is a horrible emotional weight to carry on your shoulders all the time. It weighs you right down. I felt I could never really be myself around people. I hated that so much. I resented the lads who were able to just enjoy this amazing experience we were all having.

Over the weeks in Australia I performed pretty well in the matches but by the end of the tournament I was held together with tape and bandages. At this stage I had incurred so many injuries that each one distracted from the other. I didn't know which one to focus on. A blood infection in my elbow, a shoulder I couldn't raise, a twisted knee, a botched ankle: I could take my pick. What is more, my head was fried from lack of sleep. It takes a lot of energy to disguise your mental distress but talking about it just was not an option. I thought to myself, surely I would be dropped if I told the manager.

We played South Africa in the last match in one of the most thrilling games I had ever been a part of. We were victorious by 43 points to 42, an insane scoreline. After the game we celebrated in the dressing room and my coach informed me that Leinster were going to formally offer me a three-year professional contract. It was everything I had worked towards, it was my dream and something I knew would make my family so proud. But inside I was numb, devoid of any sense of achievement. I went into the toilets in the dressing room and cried quietly for 15 minutes. I always thought this moment would be marked with champagne and deep self-satisfaction but that day it meant nothing. My private struggles had started to overpower the joy I got from playing rugby. This antidote I had used for so long was starting to lose its potency and I continued to let myself be consumed by my sickness.

Nowadays, elite rugby players in Ireland are given at least a four-week period of complete rest at the end of the season. But things were different then, and I was back in training camp a few days after returning from Australia, and picked to play in a pre-season friendly for Leinster against Connacht in Athlone. Twenty minutes into the game I got a pain in my lower abdomen muscle that felt like I had just been shot. The excruciating pain darted down the front of my legs but I continued to play on, petrified that I would be taken off in my first appearance with Leinster. It was almost as if my upper body became detached from my legs and I had lost all control. It was a pain I had never experienced before but somehow, I managed to get through the game. Adrenaline is a worryingly powerful thing.

After the match I approached our physio, Frances, to explain to her what had happened. In as calm a voice as I could manage, I told her I felt like my legs were detached from my body. It was physical pain I had never felt before. I pretended it wasn't anything to worry about but in the back of my head I knew I was in deep trouble. Frances's look of concern was a giveaway to how grave the injury was. That week I was referred to a groin specialist, the Meath GAA legend Gerry McEntee. It didn't take Gerry long to tell me that it was a double hernia and would require surgery to fix it. He told me I could attempt to play out the season with the injury but that would mean heavy painkilling medication before training and matches. There was no way on this earth that only a few weeks into my professional rugby career I was going in for surgery.

I blamed myself for the injury and masked the true extent – in fairness, had the IRFU known, they would have rested me after the World Cup. This was a complete burnout injury, nothing more.

I struggled through my first season with Leinster. With my body so battered, I felt like a taximan with no car. Here I was, training and playing with my idols, and I was embarrassed that I could not show them what I was capable of. It was incredibly frustrating and I went through some exceptionally dark and lonely times that year. I was munching down on anti-inflammatories like they were Smarties, just to get through a training session. I used to have to attach a piece of rope to the desk in the room so I could pull myself out of bed in the mornings, because of the acute and incapacitating pain in my lower abdomen muscles. I had to stop kidding myself. I needed surgery.

I remember Dad driving me home to Mullingar after the operation. I sneezed in the car, only to feel a handful of the stitches burst from the surgery. Having had a hundred stitches in my lower abdomen and groin muscles, any movements or laughter were horrifically painful, so lying in bed watching *Only Fools and Horses* reruns, as I proceeded to do, was far from ideal. I was out of action for eight to ten weeks and would miss the remainder of the season. Part of me was relieved as I was able to put my body out of its misery and hopefully come back stronger. I had an intense rehab programme as

I had to rebuild and re-strengthen the layers of muscles that had been cut through in the surgery.

Leinster won the inaugural Celtic League that season, beating Munster at Lansdowne Road after Eric Miller was sent off for dangerous play. I watched with the rest of the squad and promised myself I would do everything within my power to regain my form and play out of my skin the following season, show these guys why I was given a professional contract in the first place. It had been a very difficult year for me and one where I struggled both mentally and physically. Unfortunately, this really was just the start of it.

That summer I went on holidays to Ayia Napa with 15 of my mates from home. These school friends had followed their own paths and it was refreshing to be released from my intensive world into theirs – a world I liked to perceive as ordinary, easily navigated. As you can imagine, we were not planning on playing board games and taking wind-swept walks on the Cypriot beaches. From the minute we stepped onto the plane at Dublin Airport till the minute we returned, we were on it. I don't believe we slept for the first 48 hours, and so two days into the holiday when we ended up in a nightclub called River Reggae, I was not in the best of shape.

It was an outdoor club with a swimming pool and there were all sorts of non-swimming-related activities going on in the water. Some of us were drinking cocktails out of a coconut which had God knows what inside it, between fearlessly jumping in and out of the pool. I decided it was getting a little busy so went over to the quiet side of the pool, completely shit-faced and oblivious to the signs that said 'Shallow End', numbed with drink to my usual fear of water.

Looking back now, I realise that the self-destructive streak that had first come into being that night, years earlier, when I had broken my arm could hit like lightning at any given moment. My tendency towards physical injury or self-harm were two sides of the same coin – the self-harm a way of somehow coping with the demons inside; the injuries I picked up with alarming regularity an inevitable side-effect of the imbalances the demons caused in my life, from not eating properly to not sleeping to drinking too much. And, perhaps inevitably given the ideal storm our jaunt abroad had created, I was about to career headlong into another injury, this one my most serious to date. So, stupidly drunk and in some sudden bid to escape to a quieter part of the pool, I tried out an adventurous back-flip into the shallow end.

I could have guessed everything was not okay from the unbelievable pain of smashing my face against the bottom of the pool, but lest there was any doubt, the looks on my friends' faces made everything abundantly clear, suggesting to me that I had just been attacked by a great white shark. My ears rang. Before I knew it I was lying in a hospital bed with two doctors standing over me stitching my face, making judgemental grunts and groans about the stupid drunk Irishman in front of them. My ears were still ringing like the Angelus, stifling all other sounds in that room. Not that it mattered, because I couldn't understand a word the doctors were saying. My best mate Butch came to the hospital and stayed with me overnight. God help him, he was the drunkest man in Cyprus and he had to read my insurance details out to the receptionist while also attempting to chat her up.

They kept me in for two nights. I didn't have the bottle to ring my mother to tell her what had happened. Here I was in Ayia Napa, lying in another hospital bed, lucky to be alive after having come here to recover from surgery.

When they let me out they warned me not to consume alcohol or try to dive into another shallow end as I was on heavy medication. That afternoon Ireland were playing Germany in the soccer World Cup and we went to the Irish bar in town. I could only get a seat directly under the TV because the bar was packed, so I could barely see the match. Germany had scored and Ireland were flagging, so it felt like, rather than watch the match, the whole place was looking at the long Irish fella who had dived into the shallow end of a pool and almost decapitated himself, now drinking MiWadi and feeling sorry for himself. Suddenly, with time almost up, Robbie

Keane belted home the equaliser. The pub erupted and I sprang to my feet in delight only to smash my head on the shelf under the TV. It was at this stage I asked the lads to bring me to the vet and put me down.

As D:Ream once annoyingly suggested, things could only get better.

5. It's all about the music

A WEEK AFTER I RETURNED from my head-butting adventures in the swimming pool, I was facing into my first real pre-season programme as a professional athlete with Leinster. This is the intense training period before the actual playing season begins and it is most athletes' nightmare. I already had some explaining to do to my coaches, Matt Williams and Willie Anderson, regarding the state I was in. In my drunken plunge I concussed myself and badly cut my face, burst my lip and chipped teeth. Coming home, I still had 20-odd stitches across my forehead and a seriously swollen jaw. Since I had spent the previous season constantly injured and returning for duty looking like Sloth from *The Goonies*, I am not sure how pleased the coaches were with their investment when I told them what had happened. To be fair to them they took it well and explained that they had a lot of faith in my ability and this was the season to show it.

The first few training sessions of pre-season are physically torturous. The hardcore fitness routines would leave your lungs driving blood up into your throat, daring you to vomit, while the weights sessions were so demanding that I would be unable to dry myself after a shower, or even put on my clothes. I would just stand in the dressing room butt-naked till I dried naturally. During the pitch sessions we would mercilessly kick the shite out of each other and destroy any energy we might have left. My coaches wanted me to put on weight so they demanded I eat a sliced pan a day. This was a little while before performance science and nutrition became more prevalent in professional rugby. For dinner, I would have one plate for meat, one plate for vegetables and another plate for potatoes or pasta. I thought I had trained hard in the past, but this was all new to me. I was a mongrel sportsman, a rugby player from a Gaelic-playing school in the midlands. I hadn't prepared for something that was a hobby becoming a job and suddenly, I was playing on the same squad as elite professional players, the Brian O'Driscolls and Gordon D'Arcys of this world. I sure felt embarrassed at times about how little I knew.

On the plus side, my issues with insomnia were well and truly parked when I was in exhaustive pre-season training. Apart from the seven-inch scars on either side of my abdomen, I was showing no major effects from my operation a few months previously. I was always a fast gainer when it came to training and four weeks into pre-season I was faster, more powerful and stronger than I had ever felt in the past. Finally, I thought to myself, I was beginning to show my coaches and fellow professionals what I was given a contract for.

One afternoon, after a particularly gruelling pitch session in the blistering July heat, the squad decided to have an impromptu game of tag rugby to warm down. Although it was a bit of fun, privately, we took it very seriously, unwilling to park our egos. It was all about winning. I was really noticing that my pace and agility had improved dramatically and I was pinning the ears back every time I received a pass. I felt amazing, confidence oozed through my veins, something I was not overly accustomed to. With about five minutes remaining I took a pass and side-stepped an opposition player, leaving him for dead, as I took off like a gazelle towards the line, with a player I was competing with for position in hot pursuit. This particular player would always leave me for dust, but I was determined not to be caught so I could earn bragging rights in the dressing room. Suddenly, with about five yards remaining, I experienced the most excruciating, brutal agony I had ever felt, pulsing in my right thigh, just below my hip. It was as if I had been shot by a sniper.

I could not catch my breath as I fell to the grass in shock. I had been injured many times in the past but this time I had no idea what had just happened. All I remember is hearing a dull tearing noise simultaneous with the intense pain. The squad looked on worriedly as I roared on the ground in serious distress. Frances, my ever-present and overworked physio, had to be called in for the emergency. She gave it a preliminary diagnosis as a grade-three quad tear, potentially off the bone. My heart sank. I was very aware of how serious such an injury could be; it means a complete rupture of one of the biggest muscles of the body. In fact, it's an injury that forces many athletes into retirement. I was trying to fight back the tears but I just could not help it. I broke down in sobs on the pitch, inconsolable, knowing that even in a best-case scenario, I was out of action for three to four months.

Our bagman Johnny O'Hagan, a legend, and still the Leinster squad bagman, had a 'Run it off' kind off mentality. But after inspecting me, he didn't give his usual 'Ah sure you're all right' report. A short, brash man, even Johnny became caring when he saw the devastation in my face. Then I knew it was bad. He helped me up and had to literally manoeuvre me into the back of his van as I could not bend my leg, and he drove me back to the flat in Donnybrook I shared with three other athletes. The poor fella, I was the best part of 17 stone and here was Johnny trying to lift me up the stairs to the flat, where he left me on the couch with a set of crutches and a handful of hardcore painkillers. As I lay on the couch I could see the mark appear near my hip where the muscle was ruptured, dark with bruising. I could feel a pulse throb in my leg as it slowly turned into the blackest shade of blue. I sobbed for hours, uncontrollably, and my sobs were made worse by the fact that I couldn't reach the remote controls and some mid-afternoon bubbly shite was on the television. I felt as if I was being punished for some atrocity in a previous life, but my biggest fear was knowing that the dark cloud of depression was inevitably waiting until the shock wore off before it could descend. The physical pain would be replaced by a much more persecuting mental pain.

Unwashed in the heat of that day, and still wearing my rugby boots, I must have looked pretty haggard as slowly, my flatmates returned home from work. I had to rehash the story over and over. They were brilliant, and Kev, also a very promising rugby player, offered to go and get me dinner. Up to that point I was pretty strict on my diet in pre-season but today was different. I gave Kev €30 and told him I wanted every cent spent on the worst food he could find. Kev came back with a week's supply of chicken boxes.

I lay on the couch all night in a serious amount of pain. I was bursting to use the toilet but still unable to walk and the crutches were not of much use, so there I was, urinating into a bottle. The next morning I had to somehow make my way back to our training grounds to get a full checkup done on the injury. It wasn't good. I was sent for an MRI which confirmed a grade-three tear on my quad muscle, which didn't come as much of a surprise.

Elite sport is full of stories such as this, and yet at that time, when an athlete got injured they became irrelevant. They couldn't do their job, and no alternative was presented. I felt mistreated. I really hope things have changed. I know that within Irish rugby the Irish Rugby Union Players' Association are doing amazing things for players' welfare, both emotionally and physically. In fact, I was a member of the association in its infancy but I felt like I was thrown to the dogs when I was injured with a 'See you when you're fit again' farewell, as the dark cloud started perilously descending.

What was different with this particular episode was that I felt all sense of a future disappear. My dreams receded rapidly into the past. Before, after a setback, whether it was being dropped or getting injured, I always knew that I would manage to get back up and go again, but this time, the will that held that innate resilience was vacant, and that frightened me. I had forgotten that injury was experienced by many athletes. I couldn't see how it might be related to my mental condition, this recklessness, and felt assailed by a 'why me' feeling that only added to my sense of woe and isolation.

For weeks I lay on the couch in my shithole apartment, robbed of any motivation or pleasures. To begin with, the place was hideous, habitable purely for its proximity to UCD and the rugby pitch. It was a time capsule of faded floral seventies wallpaper, and the interior designer must have had a day off when the curtains were being picked. The sofas sprayed dust when you sat on them. You could open the front door with a credit card, the locks were so shoddy (don't ask me where I picked up that trick). Lying on that sofa, I would violently throw cups or plates against the wall in sporadic attacks of frustration. I would watch them shatter, and think what a stupid child I was – I can't imagine what my flatmates thought, but they would have sensed these red mists of rage were out of character. I was destructively aggressive and not very pleasant to be around, when anyone did break my isolation. I could not sleep at all at night as my body was so full of adrenaline, with nowhere to go. It had gotten used to the intense training and now was completely confused as to why it was made to lie on the couch all day.

Those few weeks are still clear in my memory. I was rapidly losing weight, my appetite was non-existent. My only real human interaction was with Frances, during painful rehab sessions. Some days, I could do nothing but stare at a wall for six or seven hours, lost and vacant. Or I would watch daytime television but with the sound off because, as depressed as I was, those awful chat shows really had a tendency to make you more depressed. But other days, though my motivation was all but dead, I could just about put on some of the old records I'd taken from home. It was around this time I discovered artists like Tom Waits and Leonard Cohen. I was intrigued by these downbeat voices and though I wanted to say,

'Chief, you really don't want to be pushing me now,' I did find solace in their songs.

Of course people have come through more serious injuries in the past than I was suffering, but this felt like a domino effect from body through to mind, and in harsh reality, I did not have the coping mechanisms to deal with it at all. I found myself bursting into tears spontaneously. I could have phoned my mother but I didn't want to say, 'Mum, I'm sitting here eating chicken boxes, listening to Tom Waits.' The alternative, boredom, gave me time to think, which opened doors to anxiety, which then brought on the panic attacks. My body was under attack mentally and physically and I had no weapons to fight back. I was so low. I felt as if I was letting my family down. They were so proud that I had become a professional rugby player, especially my dad, and I knew it broke his heart to see me like this. He wanted to come to the matches and say to his friends, 'There is my son,' but I was always bloody injured, and this time it looked like my dreams were drifting away from me, slowly.

This negative environment I found myself in mentally made my physical recovery much more difficult. I was not in the frame of mind to go through months of rehab again, so soon after my operation. I would lie to the medical team so they would allow me to return to training and playing. 'How is the quad, Bressie?' they would ask. 'Grand, lads, I reckon I'll be back in a week or two,' I'd reply. Like fuck I will. The one aspect of recovery I soaked up with interest was the introduction of yoga to the Leinster squad. After training, a yoga instructor called Wendy would come and work on our flexibility with us. She was so elastic we called the poor woman 'Bendy Wendy'. I found I loved the relaxation techniques at the end of the class, closing my eyes and body-scanning, though a lot of the lads just wanted to be bigger and stronger and faster, and wondered what the point of relaxation was. Obviously, my mental state was so hemmed in at this stage that I wasn't going to explain my fascination.

I rushed my recovery and decided to try to play some part in a pre-season friendly. This was just eight weeks after the injury, when I was still struggling to get up and down one flight of stairs to our apartment. I went out onto the pitch in a flurry of returned energy. Two minutes after kick-off, I picked a ball out of the back of the scrum, broke the first tackle and the pitch opened up for me. That instinct to explode onto it came as soon as I lifted my knees, at which point, needless to say, I tore the quad again.

It turned out to be an injury I never truly returned from. In the scheme of things, it finished my rugby career. I continued to play for another year or so, but never close to the promise and potential I once had. The fear of another injury constantly preyed on my mind, anticipating not just the injury itself, but the state of mind it would leave me in. Severe depression. Deep, deep, dangerous lows, and an inability to cope mentally. My depression was borne out of anxiety problems. And anxiety flourished from my inability to cope with those lows. It was your textbook vicious circle, and sport wasn't helping it anymore.

Anxiety can fixate on a problem that does not in real life exist. But in one way, my fears were realised, as throughout the season that I represented UCD in the league, I was plagued with injury. Concussions, torn hamstrings, broken fingers. I felt like a well-used punching bag. 'Why me?' I would ask to no one in particular, and then I created this simpering 'Why me?' environment. When I lay about the apartment recovering from injuries, Tom Waits muttering on the stereo, those awful American chat shows flashing on the TV, I cultivated a deeply negative pit of existence, which I dove into, inviting it to cover me over. Gradually, the sport I once loved, and needed, had become an object of hatred and resentment. It would be some time before I recognised any connection between my mental condition and my propensity for injury – how the physical and the mental are not in fact separate parts of the self that orbit around each other, but deeply connected.

During the summer of 2003, Leinster hired a new head coach in Gary Ella. It offered a slight glimmer of hope, a new leaf, a fresh start in that he might not have any preconceptions of me as a player. Since the quad tear, I had not sprinted all out. Anyone who has experienced a bad muscle tear will tell you that psychologically, it's hard to regain the confidence to sprint all out. I spent the entire pre-season under Gary barely out of second gear but he still selected me for one of our early Celtic League ties in September away to the Welsh provincial side Celtic Warriors.

Leo Cullen, a player I unreservedly respect, and no doubt one of the best professionals this country ever produced, was captain that day and I remember him roaring at me to sprint for the kick-offs, but I still felt that dull pain in my thigh as if it were about to snap. The look of disappointment on his face absolutely killed me. Here was one of my heroes on the pitch, and I was letting him and the rest of the team down. If I were fully fit I would run through a brick wall for my team but I just didn't have it in my body and it would play through my head all week after games. I was paranoid that the squad were pissed off with my below-par performances and I would dread arriving into the training grounds. I have become very aware of the negative effects of toxic environments on mental health, and this was as toxic as they came.

But I didn't have this awareness when I was 21 and determined to be a sportsman. Two weeks after the game in Wales, we were hosting Edinburgh on our home ground in Donnybrook. I knew I had to deliver a performance of some sort so I put myself under intense pressure leading up to the game. I was being paid to play this sport. In the squads and academies underneath us, there were always two or three players waiting to get into my boots and inherit my contract. I could not be perceived as weak and made to wear that label. As soon as I dropped the ball, figuratively speaking, I was gone. All week I felt a heavy weight on my chest as I fought for breath. That incessant nauseated feeling deep in the core of my stomach lingered throughout the days. These are the warning shots, and I knew what was coming next.

The Wednesday before the match I sat on my bed in my apartment wanting to tear the skin off my face. My entire body felt painfully itchy and my thoughts became like poison as they imploded in my head, loud voices of negativity. I was scraping the skin on my head so much that I was drawing blood. I kept thinking, How am I going to walk out on a pitch in only two days in front of thousands of people to play a rugby match in this state? I would have rather been injured – horrific as it was, it was nothing to the mental torture of knowing that in the eyes of others you are fit to play, but feeling completely unable.

A horrible notion came to me and I eyed the confines of my bedroom. I convinced myself that I could get around the problem if I knocked myself out. I would tell the coaches I fell, and be dropped from the team. Like years before when my urge to self-destruction had led me to break my own arm, I found myself in the grip of a similar compulsion. It was my way out – the only way,

I rationally convinced myself. So I began head-butting hard the solid concrete wall in my bedroom.

A dull ache vibrated down my neck and I started feeling dizzy. There was that sense of release, too. I am not sure how many times I hit the wall, or what made me decide to stop, but I do know I narrowly avoided knocking myself out. A grazed lump came up immediately.

That night I knew beyond any doubt that I could no longer function as a professional rugby player. I wondered if I would be able to function at all. I felt weirdly relaxed, with either a touch of concussion, or that false and temporary relief associated with self-harm. I decided that things simply could not get any worse. I rang UCD's online counselling service, and a young girl answered. I told her that I was self-harming, and let go of as much of my story as I could manage. It was a relief to offload these words onto someone else's shoulders. I fell asleep still talking to this kind girl and woke up the next morning with the phone still beside my ear, and a pulsing headache.

Somehow, I played the match, and offered a reasonable account of my ability but it was cold comfort. My career was over, every cell of my body knew it.

I rang my mother and told her that I thought I needed to retire when the season was finished. She had witnessed first hand the devastating effects injury was having on my mental and emotional health, even though we had never discussed it openly together. I told Mum that it was making me 'too upset and sad', as usual tarting up my language lest she think there was something deeper wrong with me. I think she was relieved when I told her. 'What will I say to Dad?' I asked, and she immediately said, 'Dad will fully understand.' And he did. I'll never forget how he dealt with it, he was incredible. This man who had the heartache of leaving his family for years on end understood what mattered in life, and of course appreciated that I could not do this anymore.

A couple of months later, that November, my coaches informed me that I needed to deliver a good performance against the Welsh team Llanelli at home in Dublin, in order to make the upcoming European squad for the Heineken Cup. I could not have cared less. At that point my decision was made, this was going to be my last season as a professional rugby player. Funny how these things work; as I went out onto the pitch I decided I was just going to play off the cuff and not over-think it. I loved rugby when it was raw, when it did not need to be over-analysed, but now it was all graphs and statistics, and dos and don'ts. Fuck it, I was just going to have a bit of fun in front of a packed home crowd. I literally played out of my skin, setting up two tries and running half the length of the pitch to nearly score myself, a rarity for a flanker. I was tackling players with zero regard for my safety and hitting rucks and mauls with an intensity I had never experienced on a pitch before. I was on fire, back to the old days. My coach told me straight after the game that there was no doubt after that performance that I had sealed my place in the Heineken Cup squad. I was just happy I was able to show my team-mates why I had been given a professional contract but it did not affect my choice to retire.

With retirement in mind I had to start thinking of alternative career options, potential avenues I could explore. I had been giving guitar lessons to some of my team-mates and in my ample downtime, I'd found myself writing songs, putting them on mini-disk recorders, though never letting anyone else hear them. I decided to take the least logical direction of a retiring professional rugby player, and go into music. I wanted to test those days when I'd sat in my room playing imaginary gigs and find out what it would be like to do it for real.

I started to jam with a few of my mates from back home. I was well and truly rusty on the guitar but it didn't matter, these were guys I had known for years, who shared the same passion for music as I did. We used to fire out old ska and reggae tunes in Dec our drummer's bedroom, in his parents' house. We really didn't know what we were doing. That December we approached an old school friend and seriously talented musician, Aidan Lynch, to play keyboards and guitars and almost by accident, the line-up was complete. We were writing our own tunes with no real expectations or plan, and very quickly we were offered our first gig in Mullingar. It was in the now-derelict pub Bambricks, as part of an open mic night with the local band The Cronins. We decided to give it a shot and arrived at the venue totally unprepared. We must have been the oddest-looking band, with an 18-stone, shaven-headed professional rugby player frontman. Having made no effort to dress any sharper than we did jamming in our mate's bedroom, we looked much like five punters out on a stag night. We loomed so large on that cramped stage, the people there were intimidated into liking it.

It was obvious we had something going as right after the gig we were approached by a manager and also a producer who wanted to track the four tunes we had played. Maybe we intimidated them into action as well. Later, as we loaded the gear out of the pub the snow pelted down from the heavens and we could barely see the van. From that night onwards the band became known as The Blizzards.

A week or two later we went out to the rugby club gym to record a song called 'Fantasy' with our mate Shane. The result was absolutely terrible. We had to steel ourselves to try again, and went out to Drumlish in Longford with a producer called Julian. We brought out slabs of beer and enjoyed it, still not too sure what we were doing, but our first EP turned out incredibly well. Moving back to Mullingar to make a go of it with these guys looked tempting.

Early in the New Year I had to make my rugby agent, James Adams, aware of my impending retirement. He really could not have been more supportive and in fact, when I told him about my ambition to pursue a music career, he said he shared an office with a man called Marcus Russell and I should send our demo over to him to have a listen. Wait a second, I thought, as in Marcus Russell, the Oasis manager? That was the one. Literally two weeks later Marcus Russell was at a show we were playing in the infamous Eamonn Doran's in Dublin. He loved the demo and offered to help us out in conjunction with our new manager Justin Moffat, or Moff, who became one of my closest friends. Rugby was fast becoming irrelevant in my life, although I still had a five-month commitment left in the season with Leinster. I threw myself into writing music and playing with the guys, and this offered me a new sense of purpose that I had lost over the previous few years.

I remember playing for Leinster vs Munster in early February 2004, down in Cork on a Friday night, knowing that I had a gig with the guys the following day. Injuries had struck the fear into me. I was so paranoid that I would break a finger and not be able to play the guitar but luckily I got through the match unscathed and hopped straight into the car and back up to Mullingar to prepare for the gig. Until this point I had not informed Leinster that I was going to hang up my boots at the end of the season. I still had two years left on my contract so I was unclear about how they would react. That March, I played for my club UCD in a league game against Garryowen in Limerick, using it as a warm-up game as I had been selected to play for Leinster in the Celtic League the following Friday. About 15 minutes into the game I caught a ball at the back of a lineout and was knocked to the floor. My team-mates rucked over me as I felt the full weight of a boot land directly onto my face, and more worryingly, into my eye. I remember nothing after that, apart from a vague sense of walking off the pitch with spectators grimacing at the state of my face. I apparently was trying to get back on the pitch as an ambulance rushed to the side of the grounds, where I had been hauled over to receive emergency stitching from the team doctor.

Business as usual. But this time, it dawned on me that I might have lost my eye as I could not see out my right side. Blood covered my sky-blue jersey from the collar down. I went into shock and started projectile vomiting in the ambulance as the seriousness of the situation became clear, the paramedic urging the driver to speed up. I kept roaring at the paramedic, 'Have I lost my eye?' as he pleaded with me to stay calm. As soon as we pulled into Limerick Regional Hospital I was rushed into a theatre to be assessed by the doctors. They were trying to open my eye in between my bouts of vomiting, while the nurse held a bucket in front of me to catch the vomit. It was like a scene from *The Exorcist*.

They sedated me, mercifully. As the dust began to settle they realised that the eye was still intact. I was incredibly lucky. Literally a centimetre to the left and

I might have lost my right eye. I had also suffered a pretty bad concussion and needed many stitches to my head wounds. Oddly enough it turned out to be my own player who accidentally stood on my face. When your own player starts doing that to you, you know it's time to call it a day. They kept me in overnight, but I had no clothes as the UCD bus had gone back to Dublin with my bags on it. The mother of one of the lads from the team lived in Limerick, so she kindly dropped over some of his clothes the next morning so I could get a train back to Dublin. To be fair, the clothes were a little on the tight side, so here I was on the Limerick to Dublin train, dressed in clothes two sizes too small for me, with a face like a burnt welly. My eye was sealed over with swelling. I looked like a right patch job, and I felt drained, empty. I became aware of my appearance when the ticket guy didn't dare to come near me, nor the tea lady.

Sometimes it's hard to understand yourself in any real and tangible terms. I've often asked myself over the years why I'm so prone to injury, perhaps suspicious that there's a message in there about who I am, and the condition that I have – even if I don't want to acknowledge it. On one hand it's common for athletes to get injured and hurt, but in other ways my injuries tended to be unduly dramatic and all too frequent. I was reckless without even acknowledging this consciously at the time, but I seemed to be on a headlong path to the edge of the cliff, embracing risk and ignoring danger.

Even if I knew something could lead to harm, I was the guy who would always give it a shot and spin the wheel. It appeared at times that I had blatant disregard for my body, and maybe because I resented my mind for so long, I took it out on myself physically. Or maybe I am over-thinking it and I am just the stupid gobshite that always gets himself hurt; we all have a friend like that, don't we?

The following morning, as the news filtered to my coaches in Leinster, I felt it best to go in and let them see why I could not possibly play the following week. I really was in a proper state. When I walked into the office, one of the coaches said, 'I guess you are not available for Friday so.' Good observation, I thought. I looked with my working eye from one to the other and calmly informed them that I was retiring and would not play for Leinster again. Less of a fuck I could not have given.

That autumn I graduated from UCD with an honours degree in Economics and Sociology. The day I graduated I went for lunch with my family to Wongs in Ranelagh, a Chinese restaurant I loved, though it has since burnt down. We were barely breaking apart our prawn crackers when my phone started ringing, ringing out, and ringing again. I answered. It was my old coach with Leinster, Matt Williams, who was now coaching the Scottish national team. Reluctantly, I stepped onto the street to take the call, as Matt told me he was aware that my mother was Scottish and said that made me eligible to declare for

Scotland. He asked me would I be interested in a national contract. I could not believe what I was hearing. I politely declined. Matt, a guy that was incredibly decent to me, was surprised by my decision to retire. He had offered me my first professional contract and I'll always thank him for that. He wished me the best and I went back inside to where my parents were trying to enjoy my graduation lunch, and told them what had just happened. I felt a serious sense of calm that evening, like I had cut off a cancerous tumour that was poisoning my body and mind. However, I knew that music, for the immediate future, was not going to pay any bills. I had to come up with some kind of solution.

Back at home I rang my old rugby club, Mullingar, and told them I would offer my services as a player and a coach if they found me a decent job in return. I did not feel that coming from a professional setup, the level would be too difficult, and believed I would be able to manage my injuries. The club managed to get me a job in ACC Bank in Dublin, as John, a prominent member of the club, was an area manager in the bank and extremely well connected. I was given the title Area Asset Finance Manager for Dublin. Now, I could barely spell the words Asset Finance, but I had managed to get my Economics degree from UCD, which in the banking sector of 2004 they felt qualified me for the position. They figured that given my connections with Leinster I could generate them plenty of business.

I can safely say that I was the worst employee to ever grace the ACC building on Charlemont Street in Dublin. I used to sit at the computer with a look of intense concentration as I played Snake on my phone, or wrote song lyrics on the company stationery, instead of brushing up on the tax implications of hire purchase or leasing for sole traders or companies – which I certainly needed to do. I had a default Excel sheet I would click to when someone walked past. They had got me a company car and given me a company credit card for 'entertaining' clients with. I didn't even know what 'entertaining' meant to these people. It was a case of a round shape going into a square hole. Looking back, I am glad I was not working there when the Celtic Tiger decided to move to a zoo in Germany. I like to tell myself that with my economics background, I saw the crash coming and called an early retirement on my banking career. I was getting good at this retirement stuff. I asked John could I meet him, having made the decision to get out of banking after only six months.

We sat in a glossy boardroom at ACC. As I made small talk before informing him of the decision he started writing something on his hand. I thought to myself, how rude, until he turned his hand around with the word 'Music' written on it. He knew it even before I told him what I wanted to do, and I loved him for that.

That summer I received another interesting call. We were doing cover gigs in Mullingar and commuting up and down from Dublin, but the wind down from professional sport was slow and unsettling. One day I picked up the phone to the GAA legend Páidi Ó'Sé, who was then the manager of a promising Westmeath senior team, asking me would I be keen on coming to training in the hope of making the championship squad. GAA was always my first sport. I love the passion and the simplicity of the game. I was a professional rugby player for three years and I still didn't understand the rules, but football was easy on that front, the aim being to mark your man, don't give your opposite number an inch. Páidi Ó'Sé felt I could add a bit of physicality to the squad and with my previous history it seemed like a good idea.

I went training with the squad one Friday evening, excited by the new prospect, fancying that my injuries might have calmed down. True to form, with my fitness levels down from lack of training and my vision of the sport slightly skewed, I injured myself at once, pulling my hamstring in the trial match. Tomás O'Flaherty, the fitness coach, was having none of it. His was the old school mantra, 'Get back out on the pitch, sure you'll be grand.' Will I fuck. Enough was enough. After 54 minutes of Gaelic I walked up to Páidí and told him I was retiring. A new record for me. Westmeath went on to win the Leinster senior championship that season, a huge achievement for the county that had promised so much at underage level. Everyone asked me if I was raging I did not stick it out. I just smiled and said, 'It's all about the music now.'

6. Yes we can

IDEDICATED THE ENTIRE SUMMER of 2004 to writing and practising with The Blizzards. Although I was relieved to have freed myself from the destructive environment of professional rugby, I now faced another challenge. I had no income. Having walked away from a relatively lucrative sports contract and a comatose banking career, I found myself living back at home in Mullingar with my parents, encountering a serious cash-flow problem. Cover gigs were an obvious solution, so I decided to extend my repertory of crowd-pleasers and join forces with The Blizzards' guitarist, Justin, in earning some extra cash. We got ourselves a midweek residency in Danny Byrne's, a wonderfully out-of-joint bohemian bar in Mullingar. It fell into place: The Blizzards were rehearsing in the disused nightclub above the bar, and our mate Macker was managing the place – a man with a vision, we all agreed. Of course we would.

First we were doing cover gigs around Mullingar and soon we were adding in our own songs, gigging up and down the country and gaining a reputation as a tight live act. We played in all sorts of venues, from Carndonagh on the tip of Donegal to Skibbereen in West Cork. I had so much excess energy now that I had given up playing sport and I would literally walk off stage in pools of sweat. I was enjoying this new, liberating experience and felt like I had a lot more of my life within my control. I was also enjoying being around my band mates, who I became very close to, but like everyone in my life, I never let them get too close as I was so guarded about my secrets. This is something I truly regret about the band. We spent years in each other's pockets, yet I hid so much from them, at times a thorn in the side of our collaborative effort. At times I was incredibly unpleasant to be around, aggressive and cold, almost dangerously ambitious and blindly driven, a control freak, even.

Despite the fact that our music had started going places, I found myself retreating to a familiar place of dread. The focus of my worry was money and I would lie in bed each night unable to control my thoughts or sleep, deeply uncomfortable in my own skin. Because I had no real responsibilities, I was able to just about keep the panic over my financial situation at bay, but as we gained momentum as a band, other fears raised their head.

Going on stage filled me with nerves and often, due to the erratic nature of my fight-or-flight system, would result in mild panic attacks. A pre-gig routine would involve me disappearing for a few hours to try to calm myself down. Nerves were normal for a band in its infancy, I told myself. I could not let the lads see me like this as I was the frontman, I had to hold us all together. My breathing would become irregular and I developed a nervous tick – I would grunt through my nose, like a horse. I was always on edge, and often found myself tearing the heads off people for little or no reason. God help those who had to be around me at that time.

I also found myself drinking heavily after shows as the nervous energy dissipated, putting away the free cans of beer in the dressing room before necking Guinness and, as the self-appointed life and soul of the party, I was often the last person to bed. I would think to myself, I know how bloody messed up I'll feel tomorrow, so I'm going to make it worth it. I often found it impossible to sleep after a gig unless I numbed myself with alcohol. I tried to play up the rock 'n' roll stereotype but it really did not suit me. The days following a drinking binge I would be in the depths of depression or else drinking again; neither situation was ideal. Drugs, especially weed, flowed freely backstage at gigs but I kept a distance. I noticed how chilled out it made some of the guys to smoke a joint, though through some saving grace, I knew that trying it would not be very wise given the instability of my headspace. Instead, I found myself courting Xanax on one too many occasions.

I started seeing Eva, a beautiful girl from south Dublin who was studying fashion. I met her after one of our gigs and I liked her easygoing and friendly attitude. But as soon as I saw the relationship was becoming serious, I encountered a new avalanche of worries that went with sharing my life with someone else. My first worry was my brooding personality. Eva had a jovial and sociable nature, and as my mood swings became a pattern, I grew guilty at how I often overshadowed and even darkened her personality. I remember once she called me by her ex-boyfriend's name, completely by accident. She had gone out with him for seven years so it was an easy mistake to make. I flew off the handle and disappeared for a few days in a mist of bad-feeling, refusing to make contact with her. I would sometimes on a whim go and escape to a hotel by myself, and this was one of those fuming occasions. It didn't occur to me to discuss my hurt and rage with Eva or anybody else, that that might temper my feeling. I became deeply paranoid and jealous, and found myself punching walls and withdrawing from socialising even after a gig.

My brother Ronan is a fellow musician who always had a huge influence on me musically. It certainly helped to have him as a big brother. Towards the end of the summer of 2004, The Blizzards decided to go over to Ronan and his best friend Colin's recording studio in Glasgow to record our first single, which we aimed to release in the New Year. We tracked the single over a few days and went out on the rampage, partying every night, which messed me up for weeks after we returned. Hedonism was almost written into our contract as musicians, but it made me perpetually anxious; it was the worst idea to drink at the rate we did. I knew I had to have a look at my relationship with alcohol and ended up not touching a drop for three months after I returned from Glasgow, and throwing myself into songwriting.

Warding off alcohol certainly helped clear my head and at that point I took a further step into the unknown. I started to engage in more proactive ways to manage my anxiety attacks and vicious mood swings. I found myself ringing support lines just to chat, and the comfort that gave me was unquantifiable. Isolation can be devastating. The solace you receive when you realise you are not alone is powerful. I was also much more open with my parents, especially my mother, about my breathing difficulties and anxiety. When I opened up to her it was always in muted language, using cryptic words like 'sad' and 'worried' that would match Mum's assessment that I was 'always a worrier'. Mum was no fool, she was well aware that my issues might be serious but she weighed this knowledge against my reserved personality – she never forced communication, but I always felt she would know what to say and what to do, if I needed her.

I returned to the technique of body scanning, a form of meditation that concentrates more on body parts than on breathing. It was a technique I had merely glanced at during my rugby days. You would visualise yourself somewhere that made you feel comfortable and happy while slowly relaxing each body part individually. I had always perceived meditation as something removed from reality, the preserve of hippies or robe-wearing Buddhists. But once, I was watching a documentary about meditation and a guy who worked on oil rigs was interviewed about the importance of practising meditation in his working life. He was a big, tough, all-American hero, and he said it was his survival technique. I reckoned if he could do it, I could. I started practising these body scans before gigs and it really had a fantastic effect. It's a technique I use regularly today, especially before live television.

The following April, 2005, The Blizzards decided that we would release our first independent single. The song was called 'First Girl to Leave Town', a punchy three-minute power pop track. As it was an independent release we had no real expectations, but as soon as we sent it into radio it started getting picked up by stations around the country. Perhaps this gigging lark was paying off.

I found myself working on my sister's boyfriend's farm to help bring in some cash to sustain the gigging. It was seriously tough work and being a townie, I wasn't built for the farm. A week after releasing the single, we were all awaiting news from our manager, Moff, on whether it had charted, not really expecting much. That Friday afternoon I had been given the pleasant job of scrapping the three-foot-deep cow shite covering the floor of the sheds with a JCB when my phone rang. 'Bressie,' Moff roared, 'number fucking 11 in the charts.' I could barely believe what I was hearing and questioned whether I was suffering from methane poisoning. People have asked me what I was doing when I found out about our first chart position. Well, I was sitting in a JCB, staring at a 20-foot mountain of steaming cow shit. Rock and roll.

The success of the single attracted a handful of major labels, and a few months later we found ourselves signing a record deal with Universal Ireland. I was really proud of the guys, and the work we all put in. Personally, it was a defining moment for me. I had taken a big risk, financially, walking away from a career, but after all our ups and downs we were signing a five-album deal with one of the biggest labels in the world. All we had to do now was write a record.

I was enjoying living at home, as everything moved a little slower than in the city. My dad had gone on another tour of duty in Sarajevo for a year, now as lieutenant colonel in the Irish army, so it was nice to be able to stay at home with my mother while he was gone. I was determined not to let my mental health issues get in the way of progressing the band so I started seeking out other ways of managing my mind. I took an even more nerve-racking step forward, one which today might seem like nothing but back then nearly floored me with fear. I went to my GP, Dr Healy, and told him I needed help. I told him I got breathless, that I got down. He told me it was anxiety, and said it as if I was the fiftieth person to walk into his surgery that day in the same situation, which was comforting. We both decided that medication was not required at this point. I wasn't so sure about that but nonetheless, the relief I felt leaving his office that afternoon was amazing. This time, the relief was genuine and lasting.

I loved the creative process of making our first record, working with four other guys in a sweaty rehearsal room for long hours, trying different beats and melodies until we all buzzed off the right combination. As a musician and songwriter guilty of occasionally slumping into the depths of moody solitude, nothing comes close to that feeling of collective creativity. Especially now that we had a purpose, and a confirmed album release date of October 2006.

We hired the services of the renowned American rock producer Michael Beinhorn, a man who was to have a profoundly positive impact on me. I thought I knew music till I met Michael. He had been responsible for some of my favourite rock albums of all time, including *Mother's Milk* by the Red Hot Chili Peppers and *Superunknown* by Soundgarden. I was chuffed to be working with him.

It was without doubt the most intense but rewarding eight weeks of my life. Michael pushed and pushed till he knew you were at the edge, and then he pushed a little more, better likened to a clinical psychologist than a music producer. When I played rugby, I wanted to push myself, but my body wouldn't allow it, but in the studio my emotions were open, I was in my element and revelled in the pressure to produce our music. It is astonishing how good times can co-exist with really grim times. I was also going through a terrible time with chronic insomnia. It had become normal that I was functioning without sleep and as the day turned to night, I even became more awake. I was munching down on antihistamines to try and make me drowsy every night. The band had rented a family-sized house together in Templeogue in south Dublin but I rarely talked to the guys, as I was akin to a zombie coming home every evening, praying that I would get some sleep. I never did.

I managed to avoid alcohol throughout the whole process of making the album, for a few reasons. Drinking and the shouting and late nights that accompanied it were devastating to my vocal chords and also, I knew, my head. I felt that if I even entertained a few beers something would react very negatively and I just could not afford to be off the ball. Time was money, and studios were not cheap to rent. I remember telling Michael that the day we finished tracking vocals, I was walking straight up to The Long Hall pub on George's Street and indulging in a rally of porter. True to my word, when that day came I marched towards the pub, ordered my first pint and fell asleep at the bar.

By the end of the recording process, I was a broken man, exhausted and in need of a month's sleep. Sleep was absolutely critical. Even now, without it, my head is a mess and very unstable. It's a vicious circle. Insomnia breaks down the immune system, which then leads to anxiety attacks, which can lead to days on end in your bed. The more I worried about sleep, the less sleep I would get, so I asked my doctor for some sleeping pills to try and get my head back into some form of pattern. The prescription was like a note of money, a precious currency that bought me sleep for weeks to come. Just as I started to enjoy this arrival of artificial normality to my sleep, I was flying to Los Angles, where I was going to mix The Blizzards' record with the late Mike Shipley. Let's throw some jet lag in for good measure, I reckoned.

As much fun as LA sounded, I went over on my own as the band had run out of budget for the record. What a mad city, pulsing with action from the moment we touched down over that jigsaw of neon lights. I felt completely at home in the madness and embraced the incredible weather. There was a heatwave when I arrived and people were dying with the severe temperatures. In my enthusiasm I was out lapping it up, burning my pasty-white skin to a ruby red, the way only an Irish man knows how.

I was still avoiding alcohol as I knew combining it with lack of sleep was a cocktail for disaster, but on the third night I was in the hotel and Kurt Russell walked into the bar. *Big Trouble in Little China* was one of my childhood favourite films so I had to say something. I awkwardly introduced myself by saying, 'Hi, my name is Niall and I am from Ireland,' as if Ireland were some unknown planet, in another galaxy. To be fair, I think he just bought me a drink because he felt sorry for me, but we had one or two and he said his farewells, or dodged a bullet, whatever way you wanted to look at it. Problem was, after wetting my tongue, I stayed on and got stupidly drunk with the barman. The next day I could not even sit in the mix studio without hyperventilating. Mike Shipley had worked with big bands like AC/DC and was taking this seriously and here I was, covered in cold sweats and really not in a good place. I went to the pharmacy, and to my relief, benzodiazepines could be bought over the counter. I promised myself I wouldn't touch a drop of alcohol again for the remainder of the two weeks.

That way, I could just about keep above water. I came home with the finished mixed record in my hands and there it was, evidence that *A Public Display of Affection* was to be released in two months' time. The album went on to become a platinum-selling record in Ireland and we released four singles, one of which, 'Fantasy', went on to become our biggest track. The fact that the record was well received really boosted my confidence as a songwriter and made, I daresay, all the hard work and sleepless nights worth it.

The following summer we were offered a main stage slot at Oxegen, the biggest music festival in Ireland. Everything was moving in the right direction, you would have thought. Walking onto the main stage that year, I could barely keep myself upright, so shredded were my nerves. I was vomiting in the portaloos at the back of the stage and really was not in good shape. Dec, The Blizzards' drummer, turned to me and said, 'Look at what we are about to do, not bad for a shower of boggers from Mullingar.' Perfect timing, it lifted my spirits and that day went on to become one of the most special moments in my life, where I genuinely felt a sense of jubilation, strange for me. Of all the rugby or GAA matches I played, or trophies I had won, nothing came close to this feeling of playing to 30,000 punters in that field. It was truly electric, addictive even.

The morning after the festival, as the high began to wear off, I remembered with familiar dread that perhaps the next few days were not going to be so good. With such a high came a crushing low. It was strange, as if my head was saying, 'Here, what do you think you are doing having fun?' and to punish me it made sure to let me know who was the boss. That subconscious voice was growing louder, my anxieties a ghost-like outside influence that defined and distorted my mood. I wished I had a name for it, that thing that wasn't quite my own voice but another harsh and punishing inner presence. We were due to rehearse for the coming week but I just couldn't face it. It was a new experience for me, these glimpses of sincere happiness felt with such intensity, only to be tainted by unexplainable sadness. This felt almost chemical, like there was some kind of acid in my brain that injected unhappiness. To be fair, I had heard of these crashes in mood after something momentous, but this was the first time I had truly experienced one. There was a sense that we had done the biggest music festival in Ireland, this was as good as it gets. What will you ever do that's going to beat that? An element of envy crept in, as I wished I could feel the way everyone else seemed to: grateful and content to have got this far. It took a lot out of me, this bullying voice inside, and acted as a warning shot not to ever get too excited about events and gigs, otherwise I would have to go through it again. This really was twisted logic at its most prolific.

These pretty tortuous musings were interrupted when the time came to write our second record. The idea was almost foreign to me, as it felt like we had been gigging for years and had almost forgotten how to put a song together. We wanted to be the best live band in the country, but it was important as well that we progressed the songwriting and also the sound. We were a raw, energetic, power pop band, but we needed to take that next step. Besides, I knew that if I was going to be submerged in the studio I needed to get into the right frame of mind, as I was lethargic and lacking motivation, not ideal breeding grounds for creativity. At night in my old room at home I'd lie awake thinking, until I learned it was simplest to get up and turn night into day. It helped to find something familiar and comforting to lull myself to sleep, and I'd end up downstairs having a cup of tea reading a well-thumbed Roald Dahl or an Adrian Mole novel.

Generally sleep deprived, I was struggling to put anything together musically and Michael Beinhorn felt I was leaving my personality behind in the new songs. He used to say, 'That's not you singing,' in his nasally New York accent. He was right, I wasn't in a good place and felt I needed to look at ways of bypassing how I was feeling and to write the music. We were not a shoe gaze-y, my wife left me, my dog died type of band. Not your usual malnourished indie rock band, we didn't go in for skinny jeans, skinny ties, or any attempt at a coherent style. We were the feel-good merchants of three-minute power-pop tunes. We wanted to engage our audience, and that meant we had to be like our audience. As the frontman, I had to affect a state of elation and upbeat frenzy. Quite the opposite to how I felt in the studio.

In the spring of 2008 I went to Glasgow to do a little bit of recording with my brother and put together a couple of tracks. I sent them to Michael and he felt we were getting somewhere. Over the coming months, I slowly began putting some stronger songs together that were much more in line with what we were about as a band, while still playing the odd gig. One day we were doing an afternoon show in UCD. During the sound check, our sound engineer walked out of the venue. Something was clearly up. A sound engineer would never leave just like that during a sound check. We soon realised that he had received a phone call bearing tragic news. His infant son had died suddenly. I will never forget this moment for as long as I live. Lost for words, I could not comprehend how something so cruel could happen. Over the coming days, it played around and around in my head. What kept coming back to me was that this man never got to say goodbye to his little son. I had a pain in my chest thinking about it and I just did not know what to say or do.

I thought about the family for months afterwards. Perspective is a dangerously overused term when it comes to mental health, but in this case, seeing a father lose his son in what turned out to be a sudden and horrific tragedy put everything into perspective. The self-pity my anxiety and depression brought out in me was supplanted by a sadness, for him and his family.

One afternoon soon after, I was taking some gear into our rehearsal room above Danny Byrne's. I set down my amp and next to it, my guitar. I felt a weight on my chest that had been there for days, mounting to my throat. I sat down with my guitar and wrote a song called 'Postcards' from a lyric that had been repeating in my head for days. The song was about a postcard being sent from heaven to let the loved ones know that they arrived safely and they are okay, that they will see them again one day. It was a simple idea, but let into the song it was raw and emotional. I tracked it roughly and burnt it to CD. I was really unsure if I should give the song to our engineer and his partner, whether it was an acceptable thing to do. After the funeral, they were grateful to listen to the song and later, they gave me their blessing to track the song on our record. It was some small way to preserve the memory of this little boy.

Within a few months, the album was really coming together and I gradually started building a mountain of ideas that we could move on. We were demoing tracks and sending them into the labels, only to be told, 'Great album tracks, but where is the single?' A record label executive's favourite line, but they were right. The snappy single is the marketing tool for the record, for conquering the radio and thereby paying the bills. But the thing about singles is that if you sit down and try and write one, you haven't a hope. They tend to come when you least expect it.

One evening I was getting the late bus home from Dublin. I had just been told a story by a group of mates about a holiday they were on, and how they fooled all the ladies by telling them they had amazing jobs back home. A melodic hook was hanging in my mind, waiting for a lyric to take hold of it. Staring out the window as we crossed the countryside I was singing a melody in my head that almost felt like a nursery rhyme and by the time I got back to Mullingar, literally 50 minutes later, I had written a track called 'Trust Me, I'm a Doctor'. I sent it into the label and immediately got a reply declaring, 'Now that's a single.'

We tracked our second record over the coming months

in seriously slick studios. We recorded in Grouse Lodge in Westmeath where Michael Jackson made his last music and where the Black Eyed Peas, R.E.M., Snow Patrol and other great bands had recorded. There wasn't a moment to waste. This time, I didn't just want to be a sitting duck in the studio, I wanted to learn. Days of intense conversation turned to late nights of sonic exploring, going down different avenues, talking through tempos and structure to make sure everything was on the money. As a band we shared the same vision, and felt an intense calm as we eschewed hard partying for a studio diet of fruit, nuts and seeds, replacing beer with tea and juices.

I vividly remember tracking the vocal for 'Postcards'. That weekend, my mother had lost her closest friend, Brenda, to motor neurone disease. Brenda was a brilliant character with a great presence, and it was very emotional to see her lose her fight for life. Of all the diseases I'd ever heard about, motor neurone seemed to me to be among the most horrific. A slow, staged death. First, her speech would slur, soon she couldn't talk, couldn't walk, couldn't swallow. My mother spent most days with her and, even though she refused to admit her grief, not wanting to upset me, I knew it hit her hard. I told Michael Beinhorn that I needed to go home for the weekend of the funeral to be by my mother's side. He fully understood. After the funeral, we went into our local pub to pay respects to the family. Michael rang my phone and told me to come up to Dublin that night to track the vocal for 'Postcards'. I told him that I couldn't leave my mum, but he pressed me, and my mother knew I had to go. When I arrived in the studio he told me to picture Brenda sitting in a chair beside the mic while I tracked the vocal. Michael was a producer with a very naturally caring nature, though he has a mysterious way of showing it sometimes. I visualised Brenda sitting there while I sang 'Postcards' into the mic.

Usually, when tracking vocals for albums, it can take up to 15 takes to get it right, from checking mic levels to all the other technicalities. I sang the track once through, and as I went into the control room to ask them how it was, Michael said, 'You are done. That's your take.' I thought he was having me on, but I did not realise how emotional I had become over the last few days. I engaged with every last word on the track and if you listen to the song, you will hear my voice break up in many places. I even went out of tune, but the important thing was, I connected with the sentiment. That day taught me everything I ever needed to know about vocals. Music has always been a powerful and supportive presence in my life, but one characteristic that interests me most about it is the ability to learn new things every day. Knowledge surrounding music is infinite, and if you are willing to expose yourself to other people's philosophies and methods you can discover so many other ways of expression and creativity.

Releasing an album stirs up a thick brew of anxieties.

You can release it, and straight away it can be ripped apart by some journalist. Letting your labour of love into the great wide open could have a devastating end, and we were very raw and sometimes oversensitive to other people's perceptions. I didn't take criticism, constructive or hostile, at all well at the time, and while I'd thrown in my chips with journalists – to protect myself, I decided they could write what they liked – we couldn't accept the idea of old Blizzards fans declaring, 'I don't get this.' Now we were a little bit more polished, a little less of a garage band. Due to commercial pressure, if our record didn't sell our label would drop us. I personally needed this to do well because apart from anything, it was not ideal as a 28-year-old in a pop rock band to live at home with your family in Mullingar. We released our first single, 'Trust Me I'm a Doctor', in August 2008, and it went straight to number two in the charts only to be beaten by fecking Katy Perry's debut hit, 'I Kissed a Girl'. We were just not sexy enough for number one. The album, *Domino Effect*, was released a few weeks later in September, only to be pipped to number one by one of myself and Dec's teenage heroes, Metallica. We were able to stomach that one, just about.

In October, a week before my birthday, we got on the bill for the CMJ music festival in New York City and we were beyond excited to get over and take in the atmosphere. Driving over Brooklyn Bridge for the first time was a serious buzz as we made our way into Manhattan. We were booked to play at a venue called The

Bowery the following day for an Irish music showcase. We had heard about the slick venue called The Bowery Ballroom so when we arrived we were pretty deflated to find we were actually playing in a complete dump down the street, The Bowery proper. The furniture wouldn't have been out of place in a salvage yard, and not even the PA or music equipment were going to stand our corner. Everything sounded ancient. We had gotten used to playing in pretty plum venues back home but this was a different story. Dec, our trusted drummer, was in trouble too. He had picked up a seriously bad stomach bug and was throwing up every five minutes. He looked awful, his face was see-through white, he could barely stand up straight with the pain. When before the gig I noticed he had soaked through his t-shirt with sweat I told our manager, Moff, that I didn't think it was a good idea to allow him to perform. Moff's mantra was 'If I have to stick a fire pole up his arse to hold him up, then so be it, yiz are playing.' An unorthodox but very effective management technique.

Dec was a hardy fella, but I thought this was a fight he was going to lose when I saw his white face, and the clique of record label executives frowning at us from the floor. The professional that he is, he marched on stage like he was the healthiest man in New York City, picked up the bucket left at the side of the stage for him to vomit in, threw up, and counted us into our first song. Still to this day, I do not know how he pulled it off, but when we went back to the apartment after the gig I was convinced we had to get him to hospital when I watched him have a full-blown conversation with his mother as if she were sitting in front of him on the bed. He was actually hallucinating. It turned out to be just a spell of delirium, and we let him recover in the comfort of our apartment on Chamber Street.

Later, a few of the lads and I decided to go out and sample what New York City could offer. A girl called Meghan, who I had met when mixing in LA, was living in New York at the time and her best friend Tiana was a hostess in one of Manhattan's most exclusive nightclubs so we decided to pretend we had money while Tiana brought us into the VIP section. We were introduced to a man whose name was quite simply 'Daddy', and who made me look like a kid, he was so big. I mean the guy must have been hitting 25 stone, and he wasn't overweight. It was frightening. He shook my hand and welcomed me and my 'crew' to the club. How American. It was the first time me and the guys were ever referred to as a 'crew'. We felt like heroes, me and 'ma crew'.

We had to be seriously careful about what we drank because we didn't have a hell of a lot of money and the price of drink was insane; I had decided I was not paying $15 for a bottle of beer. Daddy stood over our tables, blocking any form of light the club had to offer, and kept filling up our drinks, while I said to Moff, 'This fella is going to kill us when he realises me and the "crew" don't have an arse in our trousers.' We started chatting to a group of guys who turned out to be professional football players, so I went on a rant about rugby. They were trying to figure out how we didn't get killed without pads or helmets. I laughed to myself; if they only knew. They gave me a handful of cash, I'm not sure how much, maybe a couple of hundred dollars, and said to give it to Daddy when I was going to the toilet. This meant that if we looked after him, we would drink all night for free. I walked up to Daddy, saying nothing about the footballers and told him, while placing the cash in his shovel of a hand, 'Daddy, this is just a thank you from me and my crew,' and he gracefully accepted the wad. We drank like kings all night and didn't have to put our hands in our pockets, as the footballers sat in their seats scratching their heads, puzzled as to why they were not getting the VIP treatment. It turned out that even though they had bankrolled our evening, Big Daddy wasn't impressed with the lack of tip love they had shown him. So they didn't get such a good deal.

We fell out of the club and despite the countless warnings from food poison horror stories, I made a beeline for the street meat cart outside the club and polished off a kebab and a pretzel before being pulled into the cab home. When I woke the next morning, I was instantly aware of the ungodly fear I was about to suffer – not so much physically, but psychologically, I remembered. Before I had time to sober up I went to the local sports bar across the road on Chamber Street, with our tour manager, Ronan, and ordered a fry and a pint. Years of rugby culture had schooled me in the knowledge that if I let myself get hungover from the night before, I'd panic. I refused to let that happen. Besides, there was a lot of salt in the fry so in my imagination, we had to keep washing it down with a few pints, in case we got dehydrated.

Six hours later, having lost count of which beer we were on, it was the most natural thing in the word to pop into the costume shop under our apartment and kit ourselves out in overalls with backpacks and guns. There we were, dressed up as Ghostbusters, walking through the Upper West Side singing 'Busting makes me feel good'. We went back to the apartment to have a shower and sober up, happy that we had cleared Manhattan of any supernatural activity.

Just then, I began to get a pain in my stomach that was excruciatingly intense. Something was seriously wrong here. I sprinted to the toilet, screaming at poor Dec to get out, even though he was still no better, and I was violently ill. The pain grew like something was trying to get out of me. Whatever god-awful virus Dec was cultivating had now invited itself into my body, or perhaps it was the street meats. Jesus, it was demonic and relentless – how in name of God did Dec play a gig in this state? I was wrapped around the toilet bowl with the cold tiles keeping my burning body cool. I went through this for three days straight and I believe I actually wanted to die. The guys could do nothing except bring me a Gatorade, which never lasted longer than five minutes in my system. I was a touch dramatic at the best of times, I admit, but even Moff was concerned. The guys were all flying home a day later and I was staying. Eva had decided to come over for a few days so we could take in New York. The presidential election was also on, and we wanted to say we were in New York City when Obama was elected.

Eva had booked us into a nice hotel just off Times Square as a birthday present for me. My anxiety was in overload and I spent the majority of the day struggling for breath. When my immune system was battered, anxiety was never far away. I paced around the bedroom trying to burn off my nervous energy; I literally could not sit still and every time I lay down, my heart would race and I would start to panic. I had destroyed my body over the last week and it was now saying, 'That's what ye get, Bressie.' That vicious subconscious voice, that devil on my shoulder again. I would throw the Tylenol PM into me at night so I could quieten down my nerves and get some sleep, otherwise I would just tear my sheets in frustration. Here I was in the most exciting city on the planet, in the middle of Time Square, and I could not face going outside my room. By the time Eva arrived, I was ready to return to Ireland. She was so excited to be in New York, while I had all the appearance of a spoilt child. I really wanted to tell her why I was the way I was, it was constantly on the tip of my tongue, but I never managed to get it out.

We were right there on Time Square the night Obama was elected president of the United States, one of the most defining moments in American history. Gathered with many of the triumphant Democratic electorate were thousands of tourists who had flocked in to share this moment. There was an uncontrollable vastness to the spectacle. As the election count was ongoing and the first black president of the US had not yet been voted in, the crowd was being rallied, with helicopters overhead, hundreds of camera crews, a colossal swinging camera on a podium crane that swept across the square, news reporters rushing up to ask people how they felt. If they came near me with a camera or a mic, they weren't going to get any answers. I was like, fuck, I want to get out of here. My breathing started getting shallow. I thought it was strange that even though it was winter, I was very, very warm. I felt trapped. And I certainly was trapped, when I realised how surrounded we were.

Thousands of people had congregated. I thought, well this is a perfect place for a bomb to go off. Losing grip of where I was, my mind blew back to Israel, army tanks, bullet holes, and the sense of vulnerability in that ravaged land. Here on Time Square, the ground shook. Yes, looking around I thought, this is just the moment for a terrorist attack. I turned to Eva and, cool as you like, told her I wanted to go back to the hotel because I was sick. Eva, although disappointed, seemed to understand and we forced our way through the crowd the few steps back to the hotel. Upstairs in the room we could still hear the shrieks. The gospel songs they were singing, the chanting of, 'Yes We Can', the bawling tears of happiness. It was as American as it came. Eva wanted to be right there in the middle of it all, just like I thought I had.

Panic was landing and though I got out before it touched down, I couldn't forget that we missed being on Time Square when they announced that historic news. For a long time afterwards I was emotionally choked with the guilt that I had ruined that moment for Eva. When I got back to Ireland, I made an appointment with a doctor. I believed that I had done something to seriously harm myself in New York, that I had brought on a life-threatening disease in one of my foolish intoxications. Once again, Mum's *Encyclopaedia of Health* was coming back to haunt me, as I convinced myself I had stomach cancer or some other lethal disease. A GP in Dublin took my bloods and assured me it was nothing serious, just a bad case of hypochondriasis.

Instead of confiding in Eva, I drove her away. To protect my silence, I forced myself not to be in love with her. I was never intentionally or directly hurtful towards her, but it must have hurt to know I was keeping a secret throughout our relationship. It really felt like a secret I couldn't reveal, a great, dark shame and stigma in my society. My illness was really dictating things, as I hurt another person in my life because I could not admit to them that I was not okay.

About a year later, Eva was on tour with a big international music act, working as a stylist, living temporarily in Nice in the south of France. As it happened I was in Nice too, working with the children's author Eoin Colfer, writing a song inspired by his book in *The Hitchhiker's Guide to the Galaxy* series, *And Another Thing*. But we didn't meet up. I called Eva and we both decided it wasn't working. It turned out she was only a few miles up the road from me, where she was based for the European leg of their tour, but she may as well have been thousands of miles away. It was an over the phone break-up, after years together. I'd become so numb to losing people, I didn't even feel the need to cry.

The year after America was, to all appearances, an exciting one for The Blizzards. Though our showcase in The Bowery had been fruitless commercially, back in Ireland we won a Meteor Award in March 2009 for best live performance, and went on to support Oasis and AC/DC during the summer, and we also signed an international record deal with Island records in the UK. But although we were on the up, somehow the drive and energy that had always been our hallmark was ebbing from the band. A large part of this was because I was supposed to be leading us, but the problems I had so consistently hidden from view over the years had chipped away our friendship. Trying to plaster a serious problem with a bandage, I became ever more of a control freak with the band. In my blind ambition I wanted things done my way and no other way. As I got caught up with trying to break the UK, we were starting to become that indie band we had tried to avoid – styled, contrived, given a 'look'.

I was forcing the band to be something we were very much not. We knew Island liked us, but they had higher priority acts to concentrate on while we were still hatching our plans. When they signed a group of young lads playing folk songs called Mumford & Sons, I thought, we're done. Such is the nature of the music industry. We stopped rehearsing together and our gigs became like a job rather than fun. I had always said if this ever happened we would park it.

I never wanted to get to a stage where I would resent the lads. I had a lot of respect for them and we were always professionally straight up with each other. We all said that if the Island deal proved fruitless we would call it a day until the hunger came back and we felt we wanted to write another record. I was devastated, though. We had gone through so much together. There was so much about me that the lads needed to know. I wondered was it my fault we called it a day. Was I that much of a pain in the arse that I had terminated a career that many musicians yearn for? It felt like I'd sacrificed people's opportunities and their dreams, because I couldn't find the strength to open up. I had ruined it, I decided. In more recent years, I have put it all out on the table with The Blizzards to try and rebuild some of the bridges I tore down, explaining why I was so difficult, and the web of issues I was living with. They all completely understood and I feel we have become close again, which makes me very happy. I have had to become an expert engineer at rebuilding bridges with most of my relationships in life.

We remain friends and always look fondly upon the mad journey we went on those few years in our twenties, which hopefully one day we can pick up again in a more healthy environment. That December, we played our last gig together in one of Dublin's favourite venues, The Olympia Theatre. We gave it every ounce of energy we had to the last note, and enjoyed a few drinks together after it was all over. The mood was contrived. A sense of 'Good hustle, we gave it our best shot, shame it didn't work out.' False sentiments, plastic emotions. I went home to my hotel and cried myself to sleep.

7. London calling

I T WAS TIME TO MAKE it alone. Having signed a song-
writing/publishing deal with Universal in the UK,
and a management deal with the hugely influential
19 Entertainment, I decided I no longer had any reason
to stay in Ireland. I made the call to move to London,
a city that mesmerised and frightened me in equal
measure. Once again, I found myself running away,
hoping that I would leave my issues back in Ireland and
discover a Richard Curtis London of midweek cocktails
and fairytale love stories.

So in the first week of 2010, Moff drove me and all
my belongings over to the UK, where I would live for
the next three and a half years. The ferry from Dublin
to Holyhead was one of those terrifying crossings, as
ironically, there were severe blizzards and storms, and
the boat was being thrown around the Irish Sea, while
everyone on board tried to hold down the ham and
cheese panini they had purchased in the overpriced

ferry canteen. Maybe this was a sign, I thought to myself. Luckily, we made it to the British coastline in one piece, and endured the painful crawl to London that took ten hours, as the majority of roads were closed due to the snow. I will never forget what Moff did for me that day. He drove me over to my new home, and then turned straight back around and returned to Ireland, a 24-hour round trip due to the adverse weather. A true friend.

I moved in with an old mate from my rugby days, Eoghan, in East Putney, an upmarket suburban borough in south-west London. I was very excited to find out we were living next to Marc Bolan's old apartment – the glam rock king, and a hero of mine – but less impressed when I found out he was killed in a tragic car accident on our street as well.

The Richard Curtis London certainly didn't begin in my apartment. Being dimensionally challenged, I was actually longer than the width of my bedroom, which housed one cupboard and a bedside drawer, wedged between the wall and the bed. But it was a nice place, and Eoghan was a top guy to live with. The first few months of living in a new city are like being on holiday. Every day you experience something new, and I set out exploring this immense city in the hope that I would fall in love with its concrete charm. The sheer expanse of London unnerved me. I was aware that in order to function I would have to use the Underground to get around, but the idea of getting into a cylindrical piece of metal half a mile under the earth and then travelling off at a serious speed brought on a cold sweat of panic. There had been a terrorist attack on the transport system in central London just a few years before I moved there. It was not an option to travel by car or even bike to the vast majority of locations I wanted to get to in the city, so I had to work a way out of fear when I took the Tube. I discovered the phenomenal power of music through a technique I still use to this day.

I had been reading some articles online about how music therapy can help reduce social anxiety and other phobias, so I decided to face this unhelpful problem, to distract myself from the human crushes that enhanced my stress and anxiety. My t-shirt would be wet through by the time I was seated on the Tube, my heartbeat working overtime. One morning, I found one of my favourite albums ever, *Closing Time* by Tom Waits, put it onto my iPod, and waited. If you listen to the record, you might agree it sounds like he recorded it in his local pub, while zipping a whiskey, smoking a cigarette, serenading the barflies. Whenever I had a panic attack during the night I would play this album quietly in my coffin-like room, and imagine myself sitting in a bar listening to this incredible voice singing these beautiful songs. I was able to visualise myself at the bar, completely submerged in the music, as Tom Waits would hypnotise me with the goose bump-inducing melody of 'Grapefruit Moon'.

When I descended into the dead-air abyss of the

Tube station, I would put this record on and steady my breathing as I stepped into the train. I would then close my eyes and imagine myself in that bar, listening to Tom Waits' magnetic voice and by the time I got to my destination, not only was I calm and centred, I had also been serenaded by one of the greatest voices of all time. I literally did not get on the Tube from that day on without the company of Tom Waits. For me, *Closing Time* threw a light on how important music can be for your health, if you truly engage with it. More recently, I have been exploring the benefits of musical therapy for mental health and I feel this is a treatment that could offer a lot to people in distress. It's important to be mindful with the music we listen to. Think of the drummer hitting the snare drum, or the piano player touching the ivory keys, while the singer performs in front of the mic, rather than just the overall sound coming out of the speakers or headphones. I feel this form of therapy will continue to grow as more is learned about its potential to positively affect our mood.

London has a Darwinian, survival of the fittest, every man and woman for themselves, approach to life that can be truly overwhelming if you are not prepared for it. Moving from Mullingar to one of the biggest and fastest-moving cities in the world was a sincere culture shock. Simple things, like the constant Doppler sound of police and ambulance sirens and the occasional absence of manners in social situations, really can be overbearing for the ill-considered soul. I had to stop myself from saying 'Hello!' to randomers on streets or thanking bus drivers for delivering me safely to my chosen destination, as these people looked at me as if I had offended their mothers. Mullingar pleasantries just didn't wash in London. It can be unendurably claustrophobic and suffocating at times, but it can also be an exhilarating place to be, a place that nurtures ambition and encourages innovation and creativity.

I was signed with a great management company and ready to take up more of a background role in music, as a creative writer for new pop bands. I initially found it hard to make contacts in a fast-moving music industry which was cliquey and political. The labels tended to give the best opportunities in terms of songwriting and production to their mates and to already-proven writers. I worked with some excellent people who taught me a lot about the art of vocals and songwriting but it was still hard to make any great inroads with the bigger acts. It became more about finding unknown acts and developing them, which can be an expensive business with precious little return, unless you break the act into the industry and public domain. It could be quite frustrating at times.

By the summer of 2010, I'd been in London for six months or so, and the honeymoon period had worn off. I'd partied, I'd near burnt myself out. I recall my enthusiasm at one house gathering in East Putney with English, Americans, New Zealanders and many others, taking part in a drinking competition between the nations. We were funnelling beer down our throats using bongs, handmade contraptions like something you'd use to put petrol in your car. The object was once again to win, and to this end I became a patriot. Once I had finished eight cans of beer in 25 minutes and won this charade I realised I wasn't on holiday anymore. I was 29, engaged in a drinking competition in a dingy flat in the suburbs. Grow up? Needless to say, it was imbecilic behaviour. By the next morning, the sense of excitement I had experienced when I first moved over was replaced by concern, for how I was going to sustain myself financially in one of the most expensive cities in the world.

And also for how I was going to sustain myself mentally. Having given me a few months' grace to settle in, my panic attacks decided to return in all their previous, unrelenting glory. That taunting voice inside that told me not to enjoy myself, not to court happiness became louder and more prevalent, and I so wanted to suppress it. I was in our local pub, The Prince of Wales, one Sunday afternoon with Eoghan and a few rugby friends of his. We were sitting in the shade as the temperature was in the thirties and the London humidity was making it hard to breathe, when I started sweating unbearably, trying to disguise my shaking hands. I was soon so struggling to catch my breath I erupted out of my seat and ran for the toilet. I barely made it to the cubicle, where I lay choking for breath on the less than hygienic toilet floor. I am not sure how long it lasted but I was devastated. I had felt that maybe, having moved to London, these attacks were a thing of the past and my dark shadow had stayed back in Ireland. I left the pub without saying goodbye to the group, and made my way back to my apartment, texting Eoghan to say I was feeling sick. This constant playing down of my anxiety was really beginning to feel like deceit.

From that day on, my panic attacks returned on a regular basis, some more challenging than others. I found these attacks so disturbing I almost felt ashamed, and started socialising less, throwing myself into work yet finding it hard to concentrate. I was still developing artists and taking the occasional production fee from my studio, but essentially eating through my savings, always grist to the mill for anxiety. I was beginning to manifest physical signs of my panic attacks. Having never really had a problem with my skin as a teenager, I started to break out in severe adult acne. I would get boils on my forehead and back while the rest of my body broke out in spots and rashes. This brought on such a devastating depression I became more and more reclusive. I was put on medication for my skin which really did not help, as I was ignoring the underlying reasons for why my skin was so bad. I also started experiencing hyperhidrosis, which is when you sweat uncontrollably, in the absence of heat or exertion. This was quite debilitating. I could be on the way to meet someone and without warning, the sweat would pour from my face and body until my clothes were soaked right through. It was awful. My hair was falling out in clumps, just like I had experienced as a teenager. In the mirror I was ghost-pale, with dreadful facial acne and hollowing cheeks. These physical signs were my mental health issues made manifest and were getting me so low that I could barely leave the house or function normally.

Over the years, learning more about the intrinsic links between physical and mental health has really aided me on my road to recovery. Often we disassociate the two aspects, which is not advisable as they both affect and shape each other. On my journey it was realising the correlation between the two that helped me make the informed decisions I needed when it came to my mental health. When I am physically sick or my immune system is low, I am undoubtedly mentally low, and when I am in mental distress, I experience physical symptoms to reflect it. I start to resemble anxiety. Since I have become aware of this, I have been able to limit the amount of times I let myself get physically run down and I have incorporated actions into my life that involve the promotion of a positive physical state. I also have become more vigilant regarding what can cause my anxiety attacks or acute depressive episodes and do everything in my power to avoid them.

Avoiding bouts of depression in my life, and promoting wellness, has been about being aware of how certain situations, or actions, can affect me. Then about highlighting them and making a concerted effort to limit the negative actions and nurture the positive ones. These are highly subjective and no doctor or book will tell you the exact science of finding your triggers, but specialist advice can guide you. Ultimately, each one of us has to go on our own journey of self-discovery. Professional help when needed is very important, but the professionals cannot wave a magic wand and make all our troubles go away. I've learned from experience that if I don't make the investment in my own best interests, there's precious little anyone else can do. But once I am invested, I can manage my issues in a more effective way.

How I wish I had these inklings of self-knowledge back in London. One day we got a call from our landlord to say he would be selling the flat. The 'For Sale' signs went up and very soon Eoghan and I had to move out, finding a half-decent place up the road towards Wandsworth. There was a basement bedroom in our new flat which also contained a small room that would act as a studio for me. That was helpful as it meant I did not have to leave the house as much to travel to a studio. It also meant retreating even deeper into solitude.

At this stage I was self-medicating with more frequency. It is very easy to find unprescribed medicines when you need them. I would literally borrow, beg or steal, and always stock up on over-the-counter meds when I took a trip away. Even more stupidly, I wasn't afraid of trying what I could find on the internet. I was starting to take a Xanax in the evenings to ward off my panic attacks, but I also had my first experience of really depending on sleeping pills at night. Sleeping pills are different to Valium. Where Valium chills you out and sedates you, sleeping pills pretty much just knock you out, and this commenced my abusive journey with my sleeping pill of choice, Zolpidem. Its effect knocked me out almost instantly; even if I wanted to stay awake, I couldn't, and there was a comfort in knowing this every night when I slipped a pill from the packet. Sitting on the sofa watching TV, it must have looked a lot like narcolepsy to my flatmates, when my head would go down and stay down. I can't over-emphasise the dangers of a drug like this. By abusing these drugs I was also abusing my liver and potentially the long-term health of my mind. It's critical to communicate effectively with your GP if taking such medication, an action I failed to take at the time.

In March 2011 my American friend Meghan decided she wanted to move from New York to sit her Bar exams in London, and she came to live with us. Meghan is one of the most sincere, intelligent and decent people you could ever meet so we were delighted to have her. It was distressing, though, to find that living together was really not ideal. I hadn't known this, but since meeting her in LA I had become more hermit-like and really found it hard to engage with anyone. Meghan had an innately caring nature that I often instinctively shied away from. She did what my own mother used to do, made it clear with a glance or just one word that she was there if I needed her, and I ran from this. Looking back, Meghan was someone I should have been comfortable speaking to about my issues. But instead I disguised them and isolated myself from her, which damaged our friendship, luckily not permanently.

I was taking a sleeping tablet a night by now. Sometimes, I would wake up and take a second, in an unwise bid to avoid hours of tossing and turning, just to make sure I could get up and function the next day. By that summer I was self-medicating without regard for my health. I didn't stop, but recognising that things were getting out of hand, I decided to make contact with a counsellor. I had free public healthcare with the NHS, but I wanted to go private as I had heard quite a few horror stories about waiting lists and I felt if I didn't move fast I would let this immediate desire to get well pass. My concern was that if it was to be successful, I would have to pay something like £60 a week and I really did not have that kind of money to throw about. This is an issue that many people who are willing to seek help face. Either it's too expensive or the waiting lists are too long and, in the meantime, the support services are just not there for the number of people seeking help.

If we want to create a society where the stigma of mental illness ceases to exist, we must also create a society where our mental health services can facilitate the demand. It's often the case that people require immediate intervention, but also aftercare, if they have gone through the mental health system involving therapy, treatment, hospital. It's not a problem that can be fixed overnight but I feel we need a more long-term strategy put in place by our government to protect the emotional and mental welfare of the population. We can't always rely on the incredible work awareness groups and mental health charities do.

One of the barricades I had set up against seeing a therapist was that I would be found out. Going through the NHS recommendations on their website, I masterminded a location where I was least likely to run into anyone. I booked a therapist in Clapham – a well-known Irish neighbourhood, I was aware, but I couldn't think of anyone I knew living there at the time. Such is the warped logic that stigma creates in us. Arriving at the Tube station that morning I was nervous with excitement; I had three coffees before going in. It was the first therapist I had ever seen in person, and I believed with all my heart they would be my saviour. I had an idea of what I wanted to say and what I wanted to get from it. I did not want to regress into my past, I just wanted to look to the future, as I believed there was nothing in my past that could have had a negative impact on me – I was from a good family, a loving environment.

Within 30 minutes of the session I wanted to leave. I just wanted to rip my hair out, what was left of it. It was a small, drab room and the heat was stifling. The whale music and scented candle flickering away were enough in themselves to send me running. I remember thinking, what the fuck do you have a nutmeg candle for when it's not Christmas? The therapist, a tall and expressionless lady, seemed to be asking me the same question, over and over, and every time she spoke I was on the cusp of saying, 'Hold on a sec here, I'm paying 60 quid, let me do the talking.' She had a habit of breathing in the words 'Yeah, yeah, yeah' in rapid succession, as if to assure me of her innate understanding when really, I was convinced she was glancing at her watch every time her gaze slipped down. And so I sat there and talked, and talked and talked, the caffeine of three Costa coffees coursing through me. I suppose I wanted my money's worth, to get in as much talking as I could, but sometimes when I start to speak it can be like a ball rolling down a hill until it gets faster and faster. This lady told me to calm down, that I was a little 'manic', and turned the conversation to the bullying I had witnessed in my old school, which she then fixated on. In my head I knew that schooldays aggression couldn't have been the only reason I felt like this. I don't believe I articulated that thought. Instead, I 'machoed' up the issues – I ended by saying 'It's not that bad really,' and, pissed off, threw a pile of banknotes on her table and left, covered in sweat and visibly shaken by the time I descended into the Tube station. I had gone into the session with a closed mind and walked out with an airtight one. I felt crushed, like a wounded animal after a fight.

I want to highlight that this was a huge mistake of mine. Therapy is not an immediate solution, it takes time and an open mind, and even finding a suitable therapist doesn't always happen at once. Out of my own frustrations and ignorance I expected this lady to fix me within 30 minutes and when she didn't I lost my cool. I was like Tony Soprano in Doctor Melfi's office, a spoilt kid. I had built myself up so much to seek help that by the time I did, I had played out in my mind exactly how I wanted it to go. Some people have a skewed vision of psychotherapy. We believe it's the therapist's job to cure us, but it's really only their job to arm us with the mental capacities to deal with our issues and be aware of them. They become our coaches, but they can't run out onto the field and play the game, that's up to us. I have been lucky enough to have worked with some incredible counsellors and therapists since that day, people who have given me invaluable help and support. I have had to change my perceptions in order to understand the patient/therapist relationship in all its effectiveness.

I was left pretty empty after that day, but life was marching on. Something that I felt I was particularly missing was performing to a live audience. The buzz I used to get from being on stage really was an addiction of sorts, one that I was craving more and more. My management suggested that I perhaps look at the idea of doing a solo record, which up to that point really had not crossed my mind. I had met a talented and ambitious Irish producer, Jimbo, through some friends, and we both immediately hit it off. He was a bit of a genius when it came to sounds and production and we decided to become a songwriting/production team, calling ourselves ToyBox. Some of our early projects included working with a singer called Andrew Hozier-Byrne, who later went on to take the world by storm under the name Hozier. He was deeply shy but quietly charismatic and engaging, with the manners of a complete gentleman. I had met a lot of artists since moving over to London, and I used to ask the labels and my management, 'How do you know when someone is special, like, truly special?' They would reply, 'You will just know.' The minute I heard Andrew sing, I knew. It was a vocal unlike any I had ever heard, and so effortless and immediate.

In order for Jimbo and me to get some money to make a record, we had to put some demos together to try and get a record company to put up an advance, as we were both skint, and selling our music gear to sustain ourselves. The first demo we tracked was a song called 'You Can't Stay Young Forever', and was a complete departure from the guitar power pop The Blizzards used to play. The reality was we could not afford studio space so we did a lot of our work on synths and programming rather than recording guitars and drums in expensive studios. Within a week of sending the demo to the labels, Sony Music Ireland put an offer on the table and we gratefully accepted. We got to work on the record and managed to secure the use of one of London's premier recording studios, Sphere Studios, only a 20-minute walk from my house in Battersea.

One morning, having pulled an all-nighter in the studio, I went to unlock the entrance to the building, and as I walked out feeling utterly exhausted, I met with hundreds of screaming teenagers. As soon as they saw me, they all groaned in disappointment. To be fair, I looked rough enough after the night I'd had, but I thought to myself, that's a bit harsh. There were three other studios in the building so I presumed there must be a big artist in one of them, hence the army of teenagers camped outside. I knew the comedian Bill Bailey was in the studio too, but I was pretty sure they were not there for him, so I asked the studio manager who was in Studio 1. Barely lifting his head he informed me that a band called 'One Direction' were recording vocals. I actually got more excited than the teenagers outside. Niall Horan was from my hometown, I knew him. At 18 in London, he was blissfully innocent of how enormous that band were about to become. I rushed into the studio without knocking and greeted my new studio buddies, apologising for my abrupt entrance. It was great to see him there, and we hung out a bit over the coming days. He did all right for himself in the end anyway.

Jimbo and I made our shoestring record over the course of four weeks. It was great to have something so intense to focus on, and keep my restless mind occupied. I also got to hang out with my new band, James and Ronan, Irish guys living in London, who were two of my favourite people on the planet. Their presence had a calming effect on me and we remain close friends today. I wanted to enjoy my life now; I really watched my diet while recording and avoided alcohol as I could not afford to let myself get run down, knowing that it would corrupt my good form. I was slowly becoming more aware of myself, which allowed me to make these rational calls. I hadn't been ready for therapy but I wasn't turning my back on it, that session had opened a new avenue.

Our first single, 'Can't Stay Young Forever', went to number five in the Irish airplay charts. I had never got that far before, so things were looking up. We released 'Colourblind Stereo' the following September, which went into the Irish top 10, and received great support at radio with the follow-on singles 'Good Intentions' and 'Breaking My Fall'. I was unsure of myself in solo guise. It was odd not being with The Blizzards on stage, something I never fully got used to. At times I almost felt guilty, as if I had cheated on them. Even though we all accepted what had happened with the band, I could not get my head around being a solo artist. I missed those lads.

It seemed at this point that a lot of my anxiety issues,

guilt and regrets came from my inability to open up and talk to people close to me in my life. I had left a legacy of half-truths with people I loved and people who were close to me, and although there was no direct intention to hurt anyone, my silence left an awful lot of people confused and aggrieved as to why I was so distant at times. Some people labelled me as 'odd' while others just felt I was antisocial. The reality is, the vast majority of these people could have helped me and supported me, but I pushed them away. Nowadays we are constantly told to talk, to seek help and not hide our problems, and I one hundred per cent agree. Refusing to talk to those you love and who love you back will end up being the one regret that eats at you. A mental and emotional struggle is the most normal thing in the world, every family in every town is affected in some way by someone's struggle. If you are reading this and are still in doubt as to whether to seek help from loved ones, put down the book and make the call to someone you trust. Things will become a little brighter and make it easier for you to find your way.

During the weeks leading up to the release of my first solo album, I was kept quite busy with promotional work and gigging around Ireland. One particular day back in London, it was unseasonably warm for early September, and I felt very uneasy within myself. I was sweating profusely and my breathing was heavy and laboured, anticipating the inevitability of my impending panic attack. The waiting can often be the worst part. You try to preoccupy yourself with trivial, mundane tasks, such as emptying the dishwasher or hanging up clothes.

I was due to meet a friend that evening in Nando's. Nothing like a bit of flame-grilled chicken to rid you of your demons, but by lunch I was already listing off excuses in my head as to why I would not be able to make it.

As the humid day dragged on, I grew increasingly uneasy in myself. The sun was intensely warm and there was an eerie deadness in the air, devoid of any comforting and cooling wind, complemented by the polluted fumes of London's rush hour.

As I made my way on the short 20-minute walk to meet my mate, something came over me with a suddenness that words would not do justice to.

It was as if the lights were turned off in a room. The sun was primed in a cloudless blue sky and it felt as if I had just walked into a cave. The incessant noise of the city became muted and distant, and although I was awaiting a panic attack, I was served something entirely different, entirely new, entirely frightening.

I immediately worried for my safety and felt exposed, standing at the side of the street as cars whizzed past, unaware of the darkness that had just possessed me. Whatever was happening, it was one step beyond a panic attack. In fact it made my panic attacks feel like a trip to Disneyland. My skin felt as if on fire, and my eyes were sore and bloodshot. I would imagine that to those witnessing this, I looked extremely intoxicated, yet no alcohol had passed my lips. I think I texted my friend at that point, apologising that I couldn't make it.

There was a park around the corner which was always quiet and used primarily by well-heeled dog owners, walking their dogs and picking up their pets' shit.

I needed to remove myself from the intensity of the traffic and madness on the main street – I cannot recall which main street – so I made my way to the park, weaving in and out through pissed-off motorists, bewildered as to why some lanky drunk-looking fool couldn't just use the pedestrian crossway a few metres up the road.

When I got inside the park, I found a base of a tree surrounded by some long grass, and sat down with my head between my legs, beyond confused as to what was happening to me. I have often tried to fully explain or communicate exactly what happened that day, but logic and reason have evaded me. There was no catalyst or warning sign, it was horrifying. I started to believe that I had lost my mind, that this was the way I was to be forever. I can only liken it to those bad trips people speak of after partaking in hallucinogenic drugs, or a severe cold turkey from an opiate addiction. The day slipped into night, and I didn't move, I couldn't move. I felt safe in that spot and had no intention of leaving.

People have often asked me if, through everything, I ever felt suicidal. The answer has always been that

that was never a course of action I considered. I'm lucky enough to always have had a stable loving family, and a relatively normal life, but then so are plenty of people who, sadly, do lose control and take their life. So I don't know what leads one person with mental health issues down this road, while for another – such as me – it's not an option. I never once contemplated suicide. But during those hours, however, I did not want to be alive, not if this feeling was one I was going to have to live with. That realisation terrified me.

I stayed in that spot all night. The heat dropped dramatically and soon I was cold, resting my head between my legs but fighting sleep. As the sun came up at around 6am, I looked up to see the grass covered in a light mist, got up and made my way home through the slowly awakening streets, unsure of what to do next. When I arrived back in my apartment, exhaustion was taking its toll, but my mind was so busy with thoughts and fears and projections that I knew trying to sleep would be impossible without some synthetic help.

I took a sleeping pill and lay down. A few hours later, at about 3pm, I awoke groggy and dehydrated. My entire body still felt numb and some aftershocks were expected but nothing came. I remember having a bitterly cold shower just to try and cool down my head, to freeze the thoughts. I was just manic.

One matter that continuously crossed my mind was a

dilemma, between the absolute necessity to either deal with this or pretend it had never happened, in the hope it would never happen again. The next morning, upon waking up, it all came back to me like a horrendous nightmare, but it was all too real. It had to be dealt with, something had to be done.

8. Blind panic

THAT WAS THE IDEA ANYWAY, it had to be dealt with. But things come up, and even the most urgent matters regarding your health can get shelved and forgotten. Part of me still stubbornly believed I could solve my problems without any help from others. A few weeks before the release of my first solo record I had received an interesting call from my manager, Dougie. He asked me if I had seen the reality TV show *The Voice*. If I am being honest, I had never heard of the show but he informed me of how it worked and the concept sounded pretty interesting. It begins with what they call 'blind auditions' in which you don't actually get to see the performer, so your judgement rests purely on their vocal talent. In an image-led pop industry, this was appealing. Dougie said that TV producers in Ireland had contacted him asking whether I would be interested in being involved, and he invited me over to Dublin, expenses paid, to have a chat. I thought, if anything, it's a free flight back home, where I could see my family and friends, so accepted the invitation, thinking I didn't actually have a hope of being asked.

I met the producers in a Dublin hotel and we sat there for hours talking about the music industry, about what makes a great singer, and about my perception of *The Voice* format, as it was still a new programme. I was so passionate about music I got quite caught up in the discussion. I had such a strong sense of what I wanted that I felt at one moment that I had definitely pissed them off with my manic enthusiasm. I pretty much resigned myself to the idea that that was that, and to move on. A few weeks later, the head producer, Larry, rang my manager to officially offer me a role as a coach on the first season of *The Voice of Ireland*, which I didn't need much time to think about, signing the contract only a week later. I thought to myself, I've tried pretty much everything else, rugby, banking, farming, music, so I might as well throw television into my eclectic CV.

We were to film the blind auditions the following October along with my fellow coaches, Brian Kennedy, Sharon Corr and Kian Egan. These were internationally very successful commercial artists – unlike me, which Kian liked reminding me of throughout the show, a true friend. As a group we immediately hit it off and jumped into this new opportunity with great excitement and enthusiasm. It was a relief to be home and close to my family, to get out of London, a city which was growing increasingly more suffocating, even in the quieter suburb of Belsize Park where I had moved with some Irish friends, Shel, Kathy and Greg, top people.

The filming of the blind auditions meant intense 12-hour days of work, seeking a team of 12 singers to go through to the 'battle rounds', in which two singers were picked to sing against each other. Although I enjoyed the experience, I found it massively difficult when it came to telling singers they did not make it through and seeing their inconsolable disappointment. It was something I had to get used to fast.

Every evening when we went back to the hotel after filming I found it impossible to switch my head off, but I knew better than to drink. The first night I lay in bed awake all night and was like a zombie at filming the next day. I had procured some sleeping tablets in my usual underhand way in London and I knew these ones were pretty strong, so I decided to take one the following night. This continued every night during the blind auditions, and although I would sleep, I would wake up in the morning feeling groggy and hungover. For me, that was the lesser of two evils.

By the time I returned to London a week afterwards, I had grown so used to taking sleeping tablets I couldn't conceive of an alternative. I liked the fact that no matter how anxious I was feeling, the pills knocked me clean out. I would be watching TV with my flatmates and I would disappear into my room about an hour before I planned to go to bed to take a tablet, then sometimes fall asleep on the couch and wake up there in the morning. Because I had a doctor both in Ireland and London I was sometimes able to secure separate prescriptions, and could go through a month's supply in just two weeks. If I woke up in the middle of the night, I would just take another sleeping pill to get back to sleep, a woeful habit I had grown accustomed to over the year. If I went away for a night and forgot the tablets I would panic and not sleep, often using alcohol as the next best thing to a sedative. I could actually feel myself becoming more and more addicted to the medication, even though I was warned once by my GP that these drugs were extremely habit-forming and not a sustainable long-term solution to insomnia. I just did not care because I was able to go to bed at night and not cripple myself with worry and anxiety over whether I would get to sleep.

The battle rounds began the following November, and there I was, working as an upstanding mentor to musicians by day, arriving home shattered and taking one or two sleeping tablets every night. It was at this point too that I went to my GP in Mullingar to look into the possibility of going on anti-depressants, which can be prescribed for severe anxiety disorders. Earlier, Dr Healy had diagnosed me with 'general anxiety disorder' which certainly was a relief on one hand but also frightening, as he felt mine was on the more severe end of the spectrum.

And I hadn't even told him the full story. Basically I was afraid to, in the same way I underplayed my illness to the therapist. My doctor initially put me on a medium dosage of a medication called Effexor, making it clear to me that it can take four to six weeks to feel the effects of the drug. I had constantly fought the need to go on medication, because I did not want to be dependent on another drug. But at this point I really felt it was a requirement. I also informed my mother and father that I was going on the medication and I feel they were somewhat relieved that I was taking proactive steps for a condition I had never truly been able to discuss with them.

I waited hopefully for the medication to kick in but after a number of weeks it was still not having the desired effect. There was no apparent drop in my anxiety levels. A couple of months after this, my dosage was increased dramatically. Dr Healy kept a very close eye on me. He educated me comprehensively on how this particular medication works, making it clear that he did not intend on my staying on it forever. He would text and ring me, continuously making sure everything was okay, comforting me and making me feel at ease about the medication. I was very lucky to have a GP that took such a holistic approach to my health.

I must reiterate that it is of utmost importance for anyone in mental distress to establish a strong and close bond with their GP. They are the gatekeepers of your wellbeing and the first port of call for any issue, whether it's physical or mental. There is a lot of misinformation about medication out there and it's best to find a GP you trust and to believe in their methods, but do not be afraid to question them to the hilt to inform yourself of exactly what is happening. Don't put your wellbeing in the hands of a Google search. One of the core building blocks of my recovery was establishing an open and honest relationship with my doctor. I outlined exactly how the medication affected me and informed him of my moods at all times and he continually assessed my progress.

But there was one thing that worried me: when my doctor warned me not to abuse sleeping pills I ignored these calls. I didn't know it, but gradually I was becoming completely dependent on the drugs, and my lies were an obstacle in what we were trying to achieve. I was well aware of the possibility that my anti-depressants were not working because of my abuse of sleeping pills. Addiction breeds fear, and I was scared that if my doctor made me stop taking them, I would never sleep again. I was getting friends to get me sleeping pills and all sorts – dear God, it was completely out of control. To think, I was able to live like this for quite a long while until I saw sense.

In time, I noticed that anti-depressants were regulating my moods; they kept me at the same point, never too low and never too high. I had to be even more careful with alcohol and mixing it with the medication, though it was tricky at times, especially after a gig or a run of TV shows. I was on a very high dosage and was also put on beta-blockers to help calm me during filming, as I would often get little flutters of panic which were far from ideal when you were trying to give some poor singer who did not make it through the contest some constructive criticism.

Although we had filmed the blind auditions and the battle rounds, the general public had yet to see the show as it was all pre-recorded. It was due to be aired the first week of January 2012, which is the date when, quite literally, everything changed in my life. Up to that point, I had been in a relatively successful band in Ireland and had a few caps for Leinster, but all in all, the general public didn't have a clue who I was. The first show went out on a primetime slot on a Sunday evening, with almost 900,000 people watching it. That day I had about 5,000 Twitter followers – mostly music friends and loyal Blizzards fans – and by the end of the show this has doubled to 10,000. Some people left lovely and supportive messages, others not so lovely, but this hardly mattered, I could not keep up with it. I watched the first show with my sister and some friends in Eoghan McDermott's house, one of the presenters on the show, heading out afterwards to celebrate in my favourite city haunt, The Long Hall pub. In the pub people were coming up to me saying how much they enjoyed the show, or that it was shite, depending on their taste. You've got to love the brutal honesty of the Irish. It was crazy, and it wasn't something I was prepared for in any way.

Once you are on a family TV show, there is an element of public ownership over you that quickly becomes evident. The response was, all in all, incredibly good-natured. People wanted photographs on the street or in pubs, and I certainly did not mind, but what was quite hard to deal with was the sometimes aggressive, negative abuse you would receive on social media. I could not comprehend why people would rip your character apart under some delusion they knew everything about you having watched an hour's television on a Sunday evening. I did not like the idea that people felt they knew me, after I had spent most of my life not letting anyone get to know me. I became increasingly paranoid and on edge in everyday situations. Even though the majority of people could not have been nicer, it was the one abusive message that you always held onto, wondering why a person felt this way. Once again, totally irrational thoughts and behaviour ruled me. Cognitive Behavioural Terapy (CBT) would teach me in the future that it's impossible to control people's perceptions and it's pointless to try, but that came too late for this particular situation.

I would find myself scouring the internet for any abuse that might be aimed at me. I did not like being viewed as somebody I wasn't, but when you are in the public eye, this is something that naturally happens, I just was not prepared for it. Panic attacks, despite my best efforts, were ongoing. *The Voice* was to go live in early March of that year. I had to present a clean image on television, while all sorts of profoundly destructive thoughts were going through my mind. I had a constant fear of having a panic attack on live television. Every cell in my body felt it was going to happen, that the public would see the secrets I had hidden for so long. I believed that if anyone witnessed me having a live panic attack the reaction would either be 'Bressie is fucking nuts' or 'Is Bressie on something?' Perhaps it would have been, but it's a product of our backwards stigma that I expected this. In fact I am neither 'nuts' nor ever 'on something', I am very normal but I live in a society that labels a panic attack as something abnormal.

Very little else occupied my mind apart from the fear of a full-blown live panic attack. Would it dare to happen on television? The nausea and pressure in my chest felt like one long and muted panic attack for weeks before the first live show. I would take two or three sleeping tablets at night and sometimes, I would take a Valium to calm me down during the day. I was building myself up so much that my body was in a fixed state of sheer fear. I was so breathless that even if I was out meeting a friend, I struggled to finish sentences, as the words got caught in my chest. Alone, the slightest noise would scare the shite out of me, the smallest problem would become a crisis.

Looking at it now with a much clearer view, I can see how logic was missing from my thought processes. I was on the warpath against myself and I was my own worst enemy, but when you deal with general anxiety disorder, and it's acutely affecting you, it becomes almost impossible to behave rationally, even though you know well you are misguiding yourself. Your mind rebels against every thought and you become so robbed of sanity that you want to hurt yourself to relieve the madness. So many people in our country deal with this alone every day. Some people find it hard to believe that anxiety can become so hostile, and perceive it to be a form of stress. It's not stress, it's all-consuming fear and it pretty much takes control of your body and mind and does not give two fucks who gets hurt in the process. What's even more upsetting is that there is so much you can do to manage and deal with anxiety issues, but often people don't ask for help, they are too afraid of judgement and isolation. This is because of a stigma that is contributing to tragic and preventable loss of life in our country, week after week.

Even though at this point I was beginning to seek real help, I found myself in a very difficult situation, totally mentally unprepared for what I was facing. My environment was wildly far from ideal for someone trying to get their anxiety under control, because being in the public eye seemed to amplify the issues I contended with. I knew something was going to have to give.

The first two live shows went out on 4 March 2012 and passed off without any real incident, although I nearly passed out with nerves as we walked out each time. This was normal and everyone felt the same way, I decided. But the week afterwards, on the third show, there was an overarching belief in the back of my mind that something bad was going to happen.

On the morning of Sunday, 18 March 2012, I awoke with an uneasiness that was all too familiar. It felt as if somebody was sitting on my chest as I lay in my hotel bed, fighting back a dull and nauseating sensation, holding onto a chronic tension headache between my temples, which pushed down on my eyes. My breath was heavy and I was finding it hard to swallow my saliva, which is always a warning sign or a starter to the main course. Speaking of food, I had no appetite, but I felt I should try to get some breakfast into me. It was a long day ahead. We had a lot to live up to. On a show like *The Voice*, you live and die by your ratings of a live show. You had to create good television. There had to be tension, there had to be jeopardy, the coaches had to entertain, have a snipe at each other, have the craic – and never be boring and never, ever lose the run of themselves.

With a heavy heart and a tension headache eased by doses of water and painkillers, I sat down to breakfast in the hotel. So as to appear entirely normal, I ordered myself some eggs and took out a newspaper. But I stared at the paper, seeing only the blur of newsprint I was holding like a shield between the room and myself. When the eggs arrived, I stared at my plate, unwilling to risk eating.

After breakfast Shay, the driver for *The Voice*, picked me up at the hotel to drop me out to The Helix in north Dublin where we were filming the show. I stepped into his car and politely informed him that I was too hungover to talk. I hadn't been out the night before, but it seemed like a suitable lie. Shay loved the chat and was a proper gentleman but today, I was in no state for chatting. When we got to The Helix, I headed straight for my dressing room where I intended to hide until I was required for wardrobe, production meetings, dress rehearsal, and the other finishing touches. I was not at all well physically, either. Anxiety can feel like acid swilling around in your stomach; on top of this I had a hideous feeling that my skin was crawling with some indefinable substance, all over my body. In the bustle of the venue, no one could have been aware of this. I stepped into a bathroom cubicle and, slipping two fingers down my throat, tried to make myself sick, perhaps to make physical what was going on in my head, almost to purge the anxiety from myself. But there was nothing in my stomach.

I sat through a portion of the lengthy production meeting, keeping my head down. The excitement in the venue was palpable – the nerves of the coaches for their teams, of the producers for the coaches. I managed to avoid too much contact with others during that day. It gave me the minimum of solace to think that luckily, I had a very talented team of singers around me that had done their homework and were ready for action. Throughout the dress rehearsal I sat in my seat concentrating on trying to regulate my breathing, but I was getting progressively dizzier. The stage lights beamed through me, like a furnace on my skin. As we went through the routines I had to fake some form of interest but at this point it really felt like damage limitation, at best.

Judging a live music contest, your job first and foremost is to keep your team calm and focused. I spend a lot of time talking to my team about the psychological aspects of performing, encouraging them to sing from within themselves. Today the idea of coaching others to be calm was a travesty. I was in shards.

We were due to go live across Ireland at 6.30pm. At 6.10pm our stage manager knocked on my dressing room door informing me we had ten minutes before side of stage. She could not have imagined what was going on at the other side of that door. Just inches from her, I had collapsed, unable to breathe, spitting to the floor as I fought for air. My shirt was ripped, my ears were ringing and it appeared that the world was moving in slow motion. As panic attacks went, this was the worst I'd known yet; the idea of getting out of there only exacerbated the attack as it built, and built, and built. My brain felt like it was on fire. Tears were streaming from my eyes as I pounded my chest in the hope it would allow me to breathe again. Even half a breath, something, an anchor breath. Once you get one breath, you know there is another one coming. It is terrifying not being able to breathe, because you are certain you are about to die. I tried to scream but nothing would come out of my mouth. The situation was hopeless.

After what felt like an hour – but can't have been more than a minute – I managed to catch a shallow breath that seemed to push a small bit of air into my lungs. The anchor breath. It was enough to allow me to take a deeper breath, and another, and slowly, another, which lowered my heart rate and allowed me to regain a moment of composure. The clock now said 6.20pm.

Nothing annihilates you quite like a panic attack, no rugby match I've played, no injury I've had, no concert I've performed. When your body is forced through the crisis of a panic attack, fighting for just one breath, you are left so spent, you wonder whether your legs are actually going to support you. Slumped on the floor, I was devoid of any energy. By now, the sound engineers had knocked a few times on the door; they needed to mic me before the show, ready me for the public. Now I could hear the sound engineers being roared at by their superiors. 'Can I come in?' they were asking. 'Give me a minute,' was my weak reply, 'just another minute'. What a lazy prick, they must have been thinking. The diva, making our job harder.

I pulled myself up from the floor and looked in the mirror. It was quite a sight to behold. For those who may not be versed in television etiquette, men have to wear make-up on air, to stop the shine apparently, so at this point I had make-up all over my face. My eyes were bloodshot red and I looked like a girl who had just been dumped at the debs, or some unfortunate after a week-long binge-drinking session. Either way, I was not ready to walk out onto live television in front of three quarters of a million viewers.

Anyone who has experienced a severe panic attack will tell you it can take weeks to get over it. I had ten minutes. A deep breath was in order. I continued anchoring my breath to shore and wiped away as much sweat as I could. I promised myself that if I got through the next 90 minutes I would go about putting together a plan to change my life. I could not let my mental illness take another potential career from me. I had to dig deeper than I have ever gone during those ten minutes, the furthest back I have ever had to dig. I thought about Bumper, my six foot six grandfather, how I never left his hip when we visited them in Glasgow. I am not religious, but I prayed that he would somehow give me the strength to get through the night.

Having done a right patch job on myself, I left the dressing room and walked up the long narrow corridor towards the stage entrance. That corridor must be 50 feet long. There is a tiny incline along it. With each step of the way, I felt like I was climbing a mountain, for the weakness in my legs. I put the head down, and broke the climb into stages, stopping into another dressing room to fold my legs on the floor for a moment. It was horrible. Backstage there was a nervous energy, roaring and shrieks from the people in the green room looking for selfies and fun pictures, hair and make-up people accosting us for last-minute touch-ups. I kept staring ahead, trying to ignore it all – damage limitation.

It was 6.27, and they were fixing our mics. We could hear Kathryn Thomas, our presenter, saying, 'This is *The Voice of Ireland*, I'm going to introduce you to our judges.' I moved from sheer panic into a dream stage. I resorted to the trusted method of humming a melody in my head and as we waited behind the screen I could almost laugh, and I took in a few deep breaths.

It was so surreal, I felt drunk. For some reason, when I saw Kian Egan, I desperately wanted to tell him about what had just happened. It was too late though.

The screens went back. The room erupted, the energy rushed up with noise, lights and heat. As we joined the stage, the spotlight jumped along the faces of the other coaches, making its way to me. The last thing you want in these circumstances is a spotlight on your face. I must have been in acceptance phase, an out-of-body experience I could pretend wasn't happening. I walked to my seat, aware of the thousands of viewers eyeing me, oblivious to the hell on earth I had just experienced. Kathryn Thomas is a pro, so I am sure she noticed I was not myself. I am ever grateful to her for how she aimed questions away from me as I sat through that wretched first section of the evening. I was uncomfortably hot, the back of my top soaked, sweat dripping from my nose.

My mind had pulled through somehow, and my body was surely going to combust.

But it didn't. For the duration of the show I reverted back to the visualisation techniques I had used in the past to help me remain calm. I visualised an outcome to this secret nightmare – the end of the show, people clapping and cheering, making my way back to the dressing room. I promised myself that if I could get through the next hour and a half, I would find help, however unconventional it had to be. I bribed fate. I prayed there would not be an aftershock, which often happens. I have mentioned I am not very religious but I was also very close to my mum's mother, Granny Mac, who had passed away years before. I asked her to look over me and get me through the night.

After the show I locked myself in the toilet in the dressing room and fought back tears. I was physically depleted, barely able to walk. These days, I always make a point that people who deal with mental health issues can have an edge over those that don't, and here is an example why. Very little will come before me in life that will be more difficult than what I endured that night. When I face tough times, I always revert back to moments like these and marvel at how I managed to get through them. When I returned to my hotel room, I decided that from this night on my life was going to change. Rather than run away from my mental illness I was going to turn and face what had been beating me up all my life. I am innately competitive. I decided I was going to get competitive with this condition, and do everything in my power to find a path to recovery and regain control of my life again. I was no longer going to hide it or let it dictate my relationships or destroy my emotional wellness.

Some people call it their black dog, for others it's the clouds that block their sunlight. I decided I was going to objectify my issues, I was going to humanise them, and I was going to give my hostile mind a name. I figured that if it had a name, I could learn to get to know it, and appreciate it, sometimes my greatest enemy, sometimes my greatest friend. I was going to call it – him – 'Jeffrey', with a 'J'. It was a name I had always particularly disliked, for no apparent reason.

9. Jeffrey is born

I AM, AS I MENTIONED, one of the most competitive people you could ever meet. A desire to win is ingrained deep within me, and has proved both beneficial and detrimental. As a small child I made play into a contest, I wanted to jump the furthest from the swing of anyone; I would practise my long jumps at home before I saw my friends. At mass, I would almost push people out of the way to get to the altar first to receive Holy Communion, just to say I was first. As an athlete, losing would rip me apart and frustrate me for days. I wanted to focus this competitive streak in a much more concise and positive way, and I wanted to use Jeffrey as my competitor. I did not want it to be in a hateful or hostile way, but more in a 'You are not the boss of me' kind of way. Having run away from every other relationship over the years, I wanted to get to know myself, understand and even appreciate who I was – and this included getting to know my antagonising alter-ego. For so many years, I ran away from Jeffrey, too frightened that if I did turn and face him he would eat me alive. I was afraid that if I really went at him to try and figure out ways I could control him, and did not succeed, it would have a devastating effect on me, so my attempts were always patchy and half-hearted, as I was too proud.

In the presence of fear, I ignored anxiety – I ignored Jeffrey – hoping the irritating bollix would just go away. This is not the way to deal with mental distress. Not one of us would ignore a physical issue like a broken limb or a disease for years on end in the hope that it would one day go away. We would deal with the issue. We would attend our GP or physiotherapist and seek professional help. It's socially acceptable to do so, but due to the lethal stigma we associate with mental health issues we can often ignore them and let them grow into something more sinister and harmful.

As an introverted 16-year-old, I stood at a junction of two roads. One road would lead me on a journey of silence and fear, where I believed I was strong enough to deal with adversity on my own, while the other road was a journey of help and support, where I would be given the strategies to deal with my issues and all the inevitable crises and traumas along the way. I was unwilling to take this road out of fear of judgement and of being stigmatised. As strong as I was, no human on this planet is strong enough to deal with their mental health problems alone. It's a tough enough road even with support and guidance, so my advice to anyone suffering is, please, do not make it harder on yourself by travelling it alone. The stigma that acts like a roadblock to a more logical and safe journey is slowly but surely being knocked down, making it much easier for those in distress to seek the help they need. I cannot emphasise enough how we have to continue the destruction of this stigma, through the media, through education, through community-led initiatives and through our own self-work as individuals.

I am incredibly grateful that 15-odd years later, I found myself standing at the same junction with the same decision in front. I was damned if I was going to make the same mistake twice. This time I would do things differently.

Over the coming months, I threw myself into research and information on the various treatments, methods and strategies people were using to help deal with their depression and anxiety issues. I was not seeking a cure, I was seeking education and knowledge. I started to realise that although my issues felt entirely unique and personal to me, there was a land of people out there going through exactly what I was going through.

I started having internal conversations with Jeffrey, trying to gain some comprehension of how he worked. The things he really liked to do, and the things he really disliked. I wrote all these down on a page and decided that I needed to highlight and promote what made Jeffrey happy, and limit and avoid what upset him. Abusing my body with alcohol and bad food was out. Therapies like running, guitar and piano were in. Once I became more aware of Jeffrey, I began to look into the science of the mind – how the mind works, and in my case doesn't sometimes. I researched disciplines in psychology that interested me and made a commitment to look into some of the suggestions and treatments available. Mental health issues are far too complex and subjective for every individual to be definitively diagnosed, so I decided I would look at many options and combinations of treatments, and practise patience while doing so.

After the first season of *The Voice*, staying between Mullingar and London I experienced nightly panic attacks for months. Through my life I have had bouts of night terrors, where I would wake up in the middle of the night still half-sleeping and experience pure fear. At first I'd have a tight throat, finding it difficult to swallow. This was always the warning shot, and within a couple of minutes I would be gasping for air and in the throngs of a panic attack. It felt like I was about to walk on stage, or those moments before a big match, the adrenaline rushing through my veins as I prepared myself for what was about to happen. The problem was, I wasn't walking on stage or playing a match, I was lying in my bed drowning in adrenaline I did not need. I decided that I was going to put this adrenaline to use. I developed for myself a technique which I like to call 'the Forrest Gump technique'.

One evening I placed a pair of runners beside my bed before I went to sleep. I put on a pair of running shorts and a top as if I was just about to go to the gym. At about 2am I woke with that familiar tightness in my throat, and before I even had time to think, I jumped out of my bed and threw my runners on. I went outside, onto the empty, ghostly streets and started to run. I ran until the tightness in my throat had disappeared, burning off the unwanted adrenaline while doing so. The first morning I ran about 3km before getting back into my bed and falling back asleep for a few hours. As exhausting as this sounds, it was much more appealing to me than lying in bed and letting Jeffrey call all the shots.

I continued to practise this every night. I would wake up and just run until the dread and anxiety left my body. After about two weeks of nocturnal exercise I found myself running over 30km in just a few hours, around the outskirts of Mullingar, out towards the lakes and back all over again; I had found an inner energy, couldn't stop. The next evening I went to bed and something incredibly strange and alien happened. I woke the following morning at 8am having slept straight through the night. That may sound quite normal, but I had not slept straight through a night since I was 15 years of age.

Learning to sleep through the night transformed my outlook. It felt as if I was regaining just a touch of control over my mind and I have not experienced a panic attack at night since this day. Perhaps Jeffrey was put off by the idea of accompanying me on 30km nocturnal runs.

Before, I would turn to Xanax or sleeping pills to sort myself out, but this time I did it myself. It may sound a little over the top, and I must reiterate, this is my story and I would not encourage everyone with anxiety problems to run through the night. I have copious amounts of energy that needs somewhere to go. Once I became more aware of my body and mind I was able to look at ways of dealing with my problems more effectively. Ironically, I found out that rather than running away from Jeffrey all the time, I would run to him and meet him half way. Once I was running, I was able to relax my racing thoughts and accept what they were part of, a condition I lived with, which I now liked to call Jeffrey. I was coming to terms with that side of myself that for so many years had been a nameless, but ever-present, anxiety.

During the summer of 2012 I was still living in London but was travelling over and back to Ireland so often with gigs and appearances that it was just about manageable. I had decided to tell my ever-considerate flatmates, Shel, Kathy and Greg, about my issues. It made life infinitely easier. Prompted by countless recommendations, I signed up to an online Cognitive Behavioural Therapy course to try and grasp some of the key structures to how it worked before I committed to a CBT face-to-face session. CBT is fast becoming one of the most effective ways of treating mental illnesses and has been at the foundation of my recovery journey. It can fundamentally restructure our thought processes, which in turn affects our behaviour. Often anxiety sufferers think of the worst-case scenario, all the time, so CBT when it works can transform this irrational tendency. CBT may sound almost over-simplistic, the idea that restructuring how you think might change how you behave. But it worked for me, and helped to arm me with coping strategies that have been my crutch. I firmly believe every teenager in Ireland should be educated in CBT, as it just might allow them to rationalise and cope with a dynamic, progressive and often traumatic world.

It was some time before the benefits of CBT would begin to show. In London in particular, my tendency to panic was more aggressive. My thoughts are often my worst enemy. My head begins to race and I find it almost impossible to slow my mind down as my thoughts, which are often irrational and unhelpful, collide viciously. Sometimes my fears were picked from thin air, like worrying needlessly and without reason for days on end about my mother and father's health, among other things. Often my fears were hinged to reality, with a close eye on the plausible but worst case. When the London riots in 2011 were kicking off, we were living not far from the violence, in north-east London. Houses were being looted, streets were being closed off and I talked my mind into the idea that someone was going to come in and put fire through our letterbox. So I went off and bought a baseball bat in case someone came in and attacked me, waiting intrepidly for this hypothetical intruder. Panic feels like you lose control of your brain while it slowly fills with madness, which in turn starts affecting your body. Your heart rate increases, you begin to perspire and get visibly jittery, and then sometimes, you work yourself into having an attack.

But gradually, CBT allowed me to almost stand outside myself and monitor the situation with a much more rational approach. From here I was able to control my thoughts and regulate my behaviour. I once again dug into the visualisation techniques that had got me through the end of my hapless rugby career. I would do the opposite of what I did on the verge of a panic attack – I visualised the outcome to a situation, the relief and freedom. One method I learned was to visualise myself sitting at the side of a busy road, where the cars passing are your thoughts. What was happening to me was these cars were parking and causing a traffic jam and I slowly learned how to just let the cars pass so I could only really focus on one thought at a time. Once I grasped this approach I decided I wanted to go to a CBT therapist to further my understanding of this form of treatment.

After only four sessions with this person I realised CBT was fast becoming one of the most effective tools

I had to help manage and deal with my problems. It's a treatment I would highly recommend to people when exploring the best ways of dealing with their own individual problems, if it can be given time and patience.

Once I started to listen to myself – the darker, hidden self inside – I started to learn things. Something that Jeffrey was quite clear about was his intolerance of alcohol abuse and processed foods. They were incredibly hard on my immune system and as soon as my immune system was low, I would be buried with anxiety and depressive episodes. We can be quite naive in how we assume that what we put into our body has no effect on our moods or mental health. But our gut can act like a second brain and when we put our digestive system under pressure it can really affect our state of mind and brain chemistry. The trouble is that when we go through stressful and dramatic experiences we turn to shit food and alcohol for comfort, when it's at these times we need good nutrition the most.

I decided to have a much closer look at my diet and what I was putting into my body while cutting alcohol out altogether, to see if this helped to regulate my anxiety. I purchased a book called *The Anti-Anxiety Food Solution* by Trudy Scott and absorbed every word. I made some pretty simple changes to my diet. I prepared fresh foods and snacked on nuts and seeds, and foods rich in magnesium and omega-3 which would promote relaxation and a healthy brain function. I cut out processed foods full of those chemicals and sugars that play havoc with blood sugar levels and, therefore, mood. After a few weeks I started to notice a massive improvement both in my mood and anxiety levels. I was feeding my immune system with all the nutrients and vitamins it needed while limiting the stuff that put it under pressure. I allowed myself treats and cheat days but overall I was pretty strict with the teachings of the book and Jeffrey loved it.

Up to this point I had been poisoning myself with often six or seven cups of black coffee a day, enough to give a wax figure anxiety problems. I cut this back to two cups while substituting the rest with matcha green tea and other herbal alternatives. I was drinking three or four litres of water a day and avoiding alcohol, apart from the occasional glass of wine or few beers with mates. These changes were simple and certainly not extreme but they were very effective.

Don't get me wrong. I was still experiencing the occasional panic attack and had my down days, but they became quite rare and if I felt a particular episode coming I would make a conscious effort to stay as physically healthy as I could to try to support my immune system. Although sport had always played a pivotal role in my life, I had largely ignored it since I went into music. In truth, I resented sport due to the traumatic experiences of my professional rugby career and had no interest in embracing it again, apart from the odd half-hearted visit to the gym, or an intensely solitary nocturnal run, which felt like medicine. However, reflecting back on how I felt when I trained as a teenager and student, I realised that playing sport was an incredible support for me. I was very aware of the potential benefits of physical exercise for mental health but I lacked the motivation to incorporate it back into my life.

I decided to join my local gym and do up a programme for myself. It's really important for me that I have clear goals to focus on so I decided I wanted to get back into shape before the start of season two of *The Voice*. Not to lose weight, but to be healthier and leaner. I began going to the gym three or four mornings a week and noticed the difference both physically and mentally. That hour or two after a tough session is the most relaxing of the day and it allows me to switch off my mind for a bit as the feel-good hormones from working out hold me in a sense of calm.

The combination of a cleaner diet and good exercise was really helping, combined with CBT and various other relaxation techniques. These efforts built the foundation and motivation for my future endeavours with some of the challenges I took on.

Towards the end of the summer my record label was starting to put a bit of pressure on me to start writing my second solo record. Up to that point I felt I did not want to write an album as I was not in the right mind space at all. I had more interest in my developing relationship with Jeffrey than in songwriting, but I had a three-album deal with Sony to honour. Until now I had consciously shied away from writing about my personal issues, hiding behind a veil of uplifting feel-good pop music. The first solo record had a song on it called 'While You Are Dreaming' which was about a friend's daughter who had taken her own life, but there was nothing that illustrated my own often dangerously difficult journey. I started to play with the idea of writing about it in my songs and felt I was in a strong place to do so. I felt stronger by the day.

I wrote a song late that summer called 'Silence Is Your Saviour' which had the line 'You get what you pay for, when silence is your saviour', the most overt lyric I had ever written regarding my own mental health issues. It is an incredibly uplifting song that defined the rest of the record lyrically, and highlighted the positive progress I was making with my emotional wellbeing.

By getting to know Jeffrey, I was becoming much more aware of myself. I realised that Jeffrey was not a weakness; in fact now that we were becoming friends, I realised that he had indirectly built a powerful resilience in me, one that has become part of my character and which drives me to achieve and to help others not to make the same mistakes I made – a resilience that might help in some small way to break down the stigma around mental health that makes it so difficult for people to seek the help they require, the help that exists.

I was excited. Although this new relationship between myself and Jeffrey was only in its infancy, I felt it was a friendship that could blossom and grow into something very special, if only I could maintain the will to work on it.

10. Deep water

I MISSED MAKING MUSIC WITH The Blizzards. But writing for the second solo album had been going pretty well, and as each day passed, myself and Jeffrey were learning more and more about each other. I was still living with that uneasy feeling that this was just a phase and that after a few months I would fall back into my old ways; quite a negative approach, but after years of panic attacks and depression I felt my cynicism was merited. However, I had a fresh determination to do everything within my control not to allow this to happen. I understood there would be days I felt low and anxious, but adopted the mantra 'This will pass' for when they came on like a flu or a stomach bug passes after a few days. For years I had a conflicted relationship with anxiety attacks, angry at them, and feeling defeated, but now I did not fight the panic. I allowed it to happen, knowing that it would pass.

I might have mentioned I have a slight problem with the phrase 'positive mental health'. If someone is deeply depressed or experiencing constant panic attacks, the worst thing you can say is 'Be positive!' or 'At least you are not living in a war-stricken country'. When you're down low, the ability to be positive is virtually impossible and in my case, I don't try to be. The time that I practise positivity is when I am not feeling really anxious or low, when there are breaks in the clouds and I am in a clearer state of mind, and this was becoming a more common occurrence. Wellness is like going to the gym for your brain because it is not just about mental health, it's about mental fitness. We can all be better people, better mothers, fathers, sisters, brothers, employees, employers and friends, and by becoming mentally stronger we become more emotionally aware of those around us, and make the world a much better place to live in. The naivety we have shown in the past towards our mental capacities to deal with and manage life has created a toxic culture where human development is sacrificed for other matters perceived as more important. But those days are slowly fading out.

I had a string of solo gigs to face, and performing like this rather than as part of a band once more diced with my nerves. On 3 August 2012, just before we were due to play a festival down in Cork, I received a text from my mother telling me my sister Laura had just gone into labour, with her first child, my first nephew. We were to be on stage at 9pm, but backstage, tuning my guitar, I was barely able to stand up with the nerves. About 20 minutes before we went on stage my mother called me to say I was an uncle, to a beautiful baby boy, Billy. I never knew happiness quite like it. It was unconditional, happiness in its purest form. Playing the show, I got the crowd to sing a congratulations video for my sister. I called Laura straight after the gig and upon hearing her voice I got very emotional. I was so proud of her. I just wanted to drive back to Mullingar to hold my nephew but we had another show the next day so I'd have to wait. To feel happiness, unreservedly and without consequence, was so liberating. The birth of Billy became a catalyst on my road to recovery. Even now when I feel a little on edge, or low, half an hour in his company can lift me right back onto my feet.

The following month I was playing in one of my favourite venues in the country, The Olympia Theatre in Dublin, when I met my girlfriend, Roz, for the first time. I had heard of Roz through a friend, and seen her in the newspapers, because then she was already a well-known model. We were introduced in a bar after the gig, and I instantly felt a warmth in her character. I remember connecting to her in the strangest way. I used to be quite awkward chatting to girls, not because I had no confidence, but because I was petrified I would perhaps like them, which would make me anxious about them finding out who I really was. So I sometimes tended to come across like a bit of a shithead, a point Roz has since pointed out and proven many times since. But that night was different. She was awkward too, she gave this nervous laugh after each sentence. Together, sitting talking, we redefined awkward. But I told myself look, don't get so drunk that you can't talk to this girl properly. I went back to a party in her apartment that night and refused to leave till 5pm the following day, burning the ear off her and her flatmates. Roz and her friends seemed so welcoming and warm. It felt good to feel normal, and also to feel like perhaps if I did like someone I was in a much better place in my life now to be able to deal with a relationship, and be a much more honest and open person in the process.

Season two of *The Voice* started a few weeks later, and I was looking forward to it. I felt like I could actually embrace the experience, rather than constantly fear the arrival of my dark clouds and panic attacks. Just the year before I had just been trying to survive, whereas this year I was able for it, I wanted to enjoy it.

I wanted to learn some new techniques to promote calmness and relaxation. When I used to come back from filming for *The Voice* my head would race so uncontrollably that those weeks would unfold, when I would work myself into a panic and lie awake all night. I would think of the singers we did not put through in the show and start to feel bad for them, inviting a guilt over the possibility that I had shattered their dreams.

This time I did not want to rely on the synthetic aid of drugs to help me get to sleep, I wanted to learn how to switch myself off naturally. Although I was still on anti-depressant medication, I was slowly lowering my dosage in conjunction with my GP's advice and careful guidance, with the hope that I would be strong enough to perhaps come off meds over the next few months.

I started really engaging with the concept of mindfulness and meditation, realising that there was much more to it than I first thought. I found meditation difficult, because when I concentrated heavily on my breathing, I still tended to hyperventilate and panic – not the desired effect. I began to explore all the various techniques within mindfulness and found that there were many alternative ways to meditate. I was very patient with it. Before, if something did not work out overnight, I scrapped it, frustrated, and moved on. Like anything in this world, you must practise meditation in order to benefit from it, and since it has been around for thousands of years I presumed I had a lot to learn.

A technique called 'body scan meditation', proved to be the most effective for calming my mind. It is about connecting with your body and becoming much more aware of the muscles. We often hear the phrase 'being present' and wonder what it really means. I had to remind myself that being present is being able to enjoy the moment, to be in the now. Body scanning and other techniques such as progressive muscular relaxation and centring allowed me to become more and more present and cleared my head of the unwanted thoughts that clouded my mind.

I had always been wary of trying anything that everyone else told me would work. Initially therapy hadn't worked, and every other solace – music, sport, friendship – was a mere light on the horizon during the depths of my difficulties. I had a lot of preconceptions about mindfulness, which had held me back from exploring it, but I finally downloaded some mindfulness apps onto my phone that I would listen to as I got into bed after filming. One of the apps had an old Scottish man with the most relaxing accent slowly talking me through body scanning. I used to imagine it was my grandfather, Bumper, who had a strong Glaswegian accent that was incredibly comforting. I am not overly spiritual but I have, out of curiosity, seen a faith healer that suggested to me that Bumper is my guardian angel, and we were very close before he passed away so perhaps there is some merit in that.

Knowing that I was slowly learning the ability to switch myself off was a defining moment for me. I found myself practising this body scanning technique for just ten minutes a day and even this was clearly having an impact. When I first started it, sitting in my apartment in the evening time or lying on my bed before I switched out the light, I thought it might be pointless and it actually pissed me off a little bit, but I persevered until

I started to feel its benefits. If you have never run you cannot expect to go out and do a marathon, and it's the same with the mind – it needs to be trained and guided, so if you explore this approach please be patient and give yourself time to feel its benefits.

Along with my CBT, mindfulness was not only helping to control my mental health issues, it was actually helping me improve in many other areas of my life, both professionally and personally.

The following Christmas I had to go into hospital for surgery on an old hand injury. I'd hoped to forget having broken my knuckles in an altercation on the pitch when playing for UCD, but the baby and ring fingers on my right hand weren't looking too good. Christmas time was the only time I could get the corrective surgery done between gigs and filming for *The Voice*. My dad picked me up from the hospital after the operation to drive me back home where I would recover for the week. On the drive home, though still heavily sedated, I felt incredibly sick and fought the need to throw up. My temperature was sky high and the sweat was pouring from my face. When I got home I immediately got into bed and fell asleep, only to wake up during the night with severe sore throat and nausea. I could barely walk to the toilet to vomit and was shivering uncontrollably while wrapping myself around the toilet bowl. My throat was so sore that when I coughed, little lumps of blood came up, while I was also nursing a hand with 30 stitches in it, fresh from surgery; I wasn't even able to keep the painkillers down that were being used to dull the ache from my throbbing hand. It would all have made good raw material for a slasher movie.

It turned out I had picked up the winter vomiting bug and a severe chest infection while in hospital. This time, I wanted to curl up and disappear altogether. My mother, in her utmost discretion, didn't come into the room and try to over-pamper me as she usually did when I was at home. When you know even your mother can't comfort you, it really is a bad case. On top of the illness, or perhaps due to its debilitating effects, I became depressed and really did not want to be at home around people. At such a happy time like Christmas, you don't want to be bringing the mood down and you start to feel guilty that you are low, it's a vicious combination. I stayed in my bed for the entire Christmas period, only getting up for Christmas dinner. I was still so sick that I found it difficult to swallow or keep food down but I kept telling myself that it would pass and that in a few days I would be brand new again.

I saw a glimpse of light, as Roz and I had become a lot closer since we first met at The Olympia. On St Stephen's Day I reared my head and rang her while she was in Lanzarote, doing a triathlon training camp with her family. Her sister Rebecca was in training for an ironman, so the family had decided to make the difficult sacrifice of leaving the snow, frost, rain and cold behind and travel to the Canary Islands where they were bombarded with ten hours of blistering sun each day. They might have had the right idea that bleak midwinter. After getting off the phone I thought to myself that I would love to do a triathlon. I had thought about it before, but there was something standing in my way that made it impossible. I've had a crippling phobia of water since I was a child. I disliked swimming pools, I disliked the sea, I disliked the lakes, I dreaded fish, not God's most aesthetically pleasing of creations. The idea of an open-water swim was enough to make me bend over in a panic and it was a phobia I had no interest in overcoming. We are humans, we are built for land, fish are built for water, leave it at that.

Although myself and Jeffrey were certainly getting closer and becoming more understanding of each other, I knew that this so-called mate of mine would not like the idea of my swimming. Not a hope. So I decided to sign up for a triathlon the following summer. I felt that I needed to start pulling myself from my comfort zone and I needed a challenge to focus on, to motivate me to take even greater steps towards my recovery. That evening I committed to buying my first road bike and told Jeffrey that we were going to learn how to swim, too. He was raging.

On 8 January 2013, I had my first swimming lesson in Westwood Gym in Clontarf, Dublin. On the way to the pool I had to stop myself from asking the taximan to turn the car around. That's the thing about phobias, they are irrational and fear can shadow all sense. I knew that once I started this challenge I would be too proud, too competitive, to give it up.

Only when I got into the pool did my swim coach Carole actually realise that I wasn't over-selling my fear of water. It wasn't the water itself, it was putting my face under the water that concerned me. For so long I have had a hostile relationship with my breathing, and I think this has always been at the forefront of my phobia of water. I really did not like the idea of not being able to breathe and I panicked every time I went to do it. I just wanted to slap a pair of armbands and fins on and bob about in the water but apparently this is not allowed in a triathlon.

I forced myself out to Westwood Gym twice a week for a month, determined to get more comfortable in the water, and Carole was incredibly understanding and supportive.

Only a few months after getting into the pool for the first time I found myself standing at High Rock pier at Malahide Beach in north Dublin. I was about to attempt my first open-water swim in the chill and unwelcoming waters of the Irish Sea, and yet barely able to stand with nerves. The fear of the unknown coupled with my phobia really was a laced cocktail of emotions, but the resilience had been built up in me over the years and I knew I would not fail. It's at times like this I find myself looking back at the dark situations I've found myself in in the past, and using them to motivate me to overcome whatever challenge I faced – the years of intense insomnia, the persistent anxiety, the self-harm born of frustration. Nothing on this planet could be more challenging than those days and I believed that if I used my past in the right way it could give me an edge. These dark issues within ourselves that society might perceive as a weakness can actually become an immense source of strength. Resilience is a powerful ally.

Just as I had pulled up the zip on my wetsuit, one of the swimmers turned to me and said, 'Be careful of the seals in the bay, chief, it's mating season at the moment and they are getting fierce confused with the swimmers in the wetsuits. Just slap them on the tail if they come near ye.' I thought, what the fuck is he on about? Here I was about to face the greatest fear I had ever faced and this lad was telling me that seals may attempt to mate with me in the process. I wasn't taught how to handle this one in CBT.

I cautiously lowered myself down the steps and into the sea, keeping a close eye out for any horny-looking semi-aquatic marine mammals, and as soon as I hit the water I broke into a frantic swim stroke that had me go through the water like Michael Phelps on steroids. I am pretty sure I broke the Irish open-sea swim record as I furiously made my way out to the buoy that was 600 metres from the shore, and back again. I pulled myself up the ladder at the pier as my heart rate erupted out of control, roaring at one of the swimmers that I didn't see any seals. He calmly said, 'Bressie, there are no seals.' 'Yiz bastards!' I screamed. They simply had replaced my fear with a bigger one, mating with a seal, which put my initial fear into perspective. Cruel, but effective all the same.

I told this story once at a press conference only to see a headline on an online news site the following day declaring 'Bressie feared seals would have sex with him', with a picture of me and a seal. My mother sent me the link with a message that just said, 'Really????????'. She must have been so proud.

Having just finished recording my second solo album *Rage and Romance* in London, I was getting ready for the release date back in Ireland. I had decided at this stage that I wanted to return to Dublin. I had never fully settled in London and was starting to fall back in love with the capital. I had now been seeing Roz for a few months and I wanted to be around her more. I consciously decided that if our relationship was to become something that I would need to be really open with her about my anxiety and my past. I did not want to hide it but I also wanted her to know everything so I had nothing to disguise. Because she was also in the public eye we wanted to keep our relationship private to allow it to develop into something without external pressures from a curious public. In previous relationships I had hurt people unintentionally due to my complete inability to be honest about my problems and I was determined never to allow this to happen again. Roz was massively supportive and

I think this honesty brought us closer together. It was a really big deal for me, to share this honesty.

The album was due out on 23 March 2013 and I was pretty nervous about it. Quite a few of the songs on the record were clearly about my personal issues and questions were going to be asked by certain journalists who had listened to the tracks and wanted to know what they were about. I did not want to lie, I wanted to tell the journalists that these songs were about my experiences, that I had dealt with severe anxiety issues and depression all my life. I thought of little else in the weeks leading up to the press interviews: will I or won't I?

I thought back to myself as a 15-year-old teenager in Mullingar, choking in my bed, scared to death that I was dying, frustrated and confused and thinking I was completely alone, praying that somebody would say something to make me feel like I was normal. I thought of the desperation I felt when I bashed my arm off the bedpost until I fractured it, the hopelessness I felt when I tried to knock myself out before a rugby match, the guilt I felt when I hurt loved ones trying to disguise my anxiety, the weeks when I went without sleeping, as my hair fell out and my skin got destroyed from stress; the dark, depressive episodes that had robbed me of all emotion and energy, the crippling panic attacks I had endured behind closed doors.

The only thing standing in my way now was the stigma attached to mental illness. I had invented risks associated with opening up to people. Would I lose my job, would my friends and peers judge me or perceive me as weak, or even dangerous, would the media eat me alive, would I never get a job again, would I be mocked and ripped apart, would the trolls of social media attack my character and hence further stigmatise these issues? Weighing all these things out, I knew what I had to do.

I had to introduce Jeffrey to the rest of the world.

11. Introducing Jeffrey to the world

A WEEK BEFORE *RAGE AND Romance* was released I sat in the subdued and muted surroundings of the Central Hotel bar in Dublin, a favourite meeting place of many musicians, awaiting the arrival of a handful of journalists to have a chat about my upcoming record. I like press days. It's nice to get to chat about the fruits of your labour which you have put so much into over the previous months, but today I wanted to talk about more than just music.

There was one journalist in particular that I felt might handle the situation with the most sensitivity and compassion. Stuart Clark from the iconic Irish magazine *Hot Press* sat across from me, slowly making his way through the tracks, one by one. I always enjoyed speaking with Stuart but today I was incredibly nervous, and perhaps he picked up on this, as he suggested having a beer during the interview. Stuart is a craft beer connoisseur. Not wanting to be a spoilsport, I shared a beer with him. I noticed myself getting slightly emotional, which is never an ideal place to find yourself during a press interview, but Stuart has a very calm nature and it felt like I was speaking to a friend rather than a journalist. He noted a slight change in the direction from the last record and suggested perhaps the lyrics were a little more personal than on my previous albums. He picked up on one song in particular, 'Silence Is Your Saviour', and asked me about the background to the track. This was it, I was about to open up to the media about my past, regardless of the outcome. It felt right.

Stuart hinted that perhaps the song may have been about a friend or a loved one before I took a deep breath and told him that the song was about my own struggles and journey with mental health. Stuart, meet Jeffrey.

I didn't introduce him directly to the man himself, as it would have been a little hard to explain out of context, he might have thought it a bit odd. I spoke of my years of silence as I dealt with general anxiety disorder, the careers it stole, the relationships it destroyed and the depression it caused. Although surprised, Stuart listened with such respect and consideration, fully grasping how difficult this was for me, sensing both the cautious relief and fear in my voice. I spoke of the stigma and how the stereotypes surrounding those dealing with depression and anxiety issues were crippling and taking countless people's lives, and how it sometimes felt that we lived in a society that was not prepared to engage in this discussion. I could not help myself, everything came out. Poor Stuart thought he was coming for a quiet beer and a chat about music, while I burnt the ear off him and turned it into a psychotherapy session. I can't thank him enough for how he treated me that day. He did not see me as a television personality and musician, he saw me as a human being, something people often fail to do with each other.

When I left the interview I had no idea what Stuart was going to write. Would he sensationalise the piece, use it as the core theme of the interview, would he twist my words and further stigmatise the conversation around mental health? I left these questions when I walked out of the Central Hotel with the conversation behind me, and floated up George's Street with a sense of pure satisfaction that I had never experienced the like of before. My breathing seemed deeper and calmer, and the consistent tension that was held rigid through my body seemed to dissipate. I was completely at ease with what just happened as the world seemed to drift past me in slow motion. I have an inbuilt energy that refuses to let my body ever relax. I don't say that in a dramatic way. I find it virtually impossible to calm myself down, to a point that I cannot just sit on a couch watching television or sit by a pool on holiday. I have been like this all my life. On this particular day, walking through the streets of Dublin, I found myself, for the first time for as long as I can remember, truly relaxed, truly calm, truly happy. The past was irrelevant, the future was clear in my mind, I was completely embracing this present moment of pure calm, and it felt amazing.

In recent years my good friend and sports psychologist Gerry Hussey has educated me on the concept of the traffic light system. The idea is founded on the principle that we cannot always be in the red light zone. The red light zone is where our bodies are preparing for stress or a situation that requires full concentration, much like the fight mode of the 'fight or flight' phenomenon. It could be a big interview, a match or an exam. The adrenaline rushing through our veins preparing us for battle is of course a key aspect of survival but it is not sustainable to be in this space all of the time. For a healthy mind, it's paramount that we can put ourselves in the amber and green zones of the traffic light system. We must arm ourselves with efficient strategies that allow us enter into these zones and experience calmness and a positive state of mind. For years I found myself rigidly in the red zone, burning myself out with stress and anxiety, unable to switch my mind off. It truly is exhausting but over the years I have found ways of using this internal energy as a crucial component of my resilience and drive to succeed. However, I have also learned how to control this internal energy and allow my body and mind to relax and embrace rare moments of quiet.

A few weeks after my outpouring in the Central Hotel, the *Hot Press* piece came out. They put me on their front cover. That is a serious buzz, a dream for any Irish musician. I had to stop my hands from shaking as I flicked through the pages to find the interview, trying to talk myself out of reading it. I ordinarily hate reading interviews, listening to myself or watching myself on TV, so you can imagine how conflicted I felt about reading this one.

The first words that jumped out at me were 'panic attack', which ironically nearly brought one on, but as I made my way through the article I realised that Stuart had penned a piece that could not have been more on the money. He didn't spin my words, he did not run with sensationalised headlines or over-dramatised experiences, he didn't balance his writing on lazy and stigmatising stereotypes, he basically made it all sound very normal and something we all have either direct or indirect experience of, which of course is true.

Dear everyone, meet Jeffrey.

Regardless of what was written, I was very aware that I would have no control over what the press on a wider level would write. I was worried at this point that the media might spin the article a bit as *The Voice*, which was currently airing, was one of the biggest entertainment shows on Irish television. Panic attacks could be seen as ideal cannon fodder for a cheap headline. But the Irish media were massively supportive and respectful. They handled my difficult story incredibly well. After all, they have sisters, brothers and mothers and fathers who could well have experienced the same issues I faced, in a society where talking and seeking help is not particularly promoted.

I won't lie, I got a small amount of abuse on social media, which of course is almost clichéd at this point. I was called a 'pussy', I was told to 'man up', I was even called a 'disgrace'. We still live under a dark shadow of stigma around this subject, completely uneducated on how that stigma can affect people from any gender, demographic, race, class or age. Being called a 'pussy' by one individual is not my concern, my concern is at a macro level. What are we doing on a strategic basis to help change attitudes towards mental health in this country? Our schools are certainly trying but it's individually based and patchy. This must change and it must become a priority of our education system, and we must not allow politics to get in the way. It is frustrating to the core when politics and economics are prioritised ahead of human development. So often in a capitalist society economics come first, humanity comes second.

Those individuals who chose to abuse me online no doubt have family members or friends who live silently in distress with depression, anxiety or other mental health concerns and the likelihood of them seeking help is very low considering the environment they live in, where their loved ones believe anyone with such issues is a 'pussy'. My informing them of their ignorance is pointless, so I didn't bother, they must be educated in time at a more profound level. Overall, the empathy and sincere support that I received both from the media and the general public in the months following the interview offered me immense comfort. For years I was silent about mental health, now you won't shut me up about it.

A month or so after the *Hot Press* piece came out I received an interesting call from a man introducing himself as Jim Breen, asking could he meet me to chat about an idea he had. Little did I know that Jim would have a deeply positive impact on my future and indeed the conversation surrounding mental health on the island of Ireland. He had a rather ambitious idea to cycle 1,400km around Ireland in 14 days with a large group of volunteers under the banner of the 'Cycle Against Suicide' and he wanted me to become an ambassador for the event. He had read the press coverage about my own struggles and felt I would be an ideal match for the campaign as I was also, at this point, a keen cyclist.

I met Jim for a coffee in Dublin and became immediately enamoured by his talkative presence and passion surrounding the subject of mental health and suicide in this country. Jim himself, a hugely successful tech entrepreneur, informed me that he had lived with bi-polar depression for years and wanted to do something about the stigma of mental illness and its related epidemic of suicide in this country. I had never spoken with such clarity about the subject as I did that day with Jim. I promised him that I would do my best to make as much of the cycle as possible, as I was still juggling the live shows of *The Voice*. I asked Dougie, my manager, to fit in as many dates as they could but after doing just one cycle with the group, I emailed back and told him to clear my diary, that I was staying on the cycle.

That first evening I arrived in Tralee to meet Jim and the rest of the cyclists. Jim suggested that he and I go to see a local teenager living with terminal cancer, who had just done a compelling interview on *The Saturday Night Show* on RTÉ the previous week about the value of life, urging young people to stop taking their lives. I sat in Donal Walsh's sitting room that evening, talking about rugby and music – Donal was a religious Munster fan and he was pissed off I hadn't signed with Munster, when I told him about an opportunity I'd had. I think we had intended to speak about mental health and the Cycle Against Suicide, but he was quite unwell so I wanted to talk to him normally, just two guys having a chat. I left that evening knowing that I would probably never see Donal again but also knowing that he had switched something on inside me. He had told me that life is precious: live it. I wanted to help carry on this message, not just out of respect for him, but also because he had opened the dialogue for the teenagers of this country when others had tried and failed, and this is a legacy that his family, friends and loved ones must be very proud of. A big hope of mine is to help develop this dialogue and keep this light that Donal sparked shining bright. I am eternally grateful that I got to meet this special teenager before he passed away only a few weeks later.

Over the coming weeks I cycled with thousands of people, many of whom openly told me about their stories and struggles. We cycled throughout the island of Ireland in weather that raged between four seasons in one day, stopping twice a day in towns and villages to meet and talk to people. As part of the cycle's remit, I got up in front of thousands of students in schools around the country and spoke of the fear and isolation I felt as a teenager experiencing anxiety and panic attacks. I spoke to small communities and also universities about my experiences. Although this was a foundational journey, I did feel at times that exposing myself at this level was having an adverse impact on my own mental health, so I was constantly aware of how I was feeling, which allowed me to eject myself from the situation if I needed to.

During one of the cycles from Sligo to Donegal town, I got talking to a couple in their early sixties about why they decided to embark on the Cycle Against Suicide. They told me the tragic story of their son, who had lived with general anxiety disorder for years and had taken his life only three weeks before the cycle. With much emotion, they replayed his life to me, talking of his crippling panic attacks, insomnia, dangerous lows and social isolation. At times, it felt like they were describing my experiences. I don't know how I held back the tears while they went through their son's story.

They spoke about how they wished they could have helped and wished they were there when he took his life so they could have stopped him. I had never heard a more heartbreaking story but I was able to relate to every word. How many men around Ireland end up in this situation because they won't seek help? How many parents have to endure the same story because we live in a country that largely ignores issues such as these?

We pulled in for some food a few miles further up the road towards Donegal town, and I could not help myself from embracing the couple as they cried. I would love to pretend that living with emotional distress and mental health issues is easy, but it's not. Sometimes it can be too much for people, sometimes people have to live with other issues on top of it all, but quite a lot of these people never seek help. Sometimes they seek help and it's not available or they have to wait months before anyone sees them. The culture and attitude towards this subject has to change. I still go to bed at night and spend the first minutes controlling my breathing and calming myself. It's part of life, I accept it and count myself lucky that I have developed coping strategies to deal with life's uncertainties, so far.

I learned an awful lot on that cycle. I knew that quite a few people were affected by mental health issues but I had never realised how prevalent they are throughout this country. I heard heartbreaking stories but I also heard inspiring and empowering stories, stories of such resilience and strength. After cycling around the island of Ireland we made our way into Dublin through the north side of the city, coming down from Dundalk. A group of young teenagers sprinted alongside the bikes, clapping and cheering as we cycled into the city in our army of orange jerseys. When we were stopping to regroup before the last lap into the city, I got off the bicycle and chatted to these teenagers to find out that their close friend had taken his own life a few weeks previously. It was a sobering moment that really defined why we were out on our bikes trying to create awareness around the topic of suicide and depression in this country.

These were experiences that opened my eyes, and fuelled my motivations to try to help change people's attitudes towards mental health. Over the years I have got used to exposing myself emotionally to people in order to help them perhaps realise that they are not alone, but it can be hard when through my story people see me as someone who can instantly help them. It has become important for me to be able to recognise when I need to step back and concentrate on myself, and become more aware of how I feel, otherwise I am of no use to anyone. So when it was all over, myself and Jeffrey needed a break. I needed to re-engage and give some time to myself.

It must be said, though, I did not have too much time to myself after the cycle. I was given the opportunity to go on Ireland's biggest current affairs programme, *Prime Time*, to speak about teenage mental health issues in Ireland at that time. Although slightly intimidating, I felt that with the audience the show reached, it would not be a bad call to just do it. It was a real sign of the appetite and hunger out there to speak about the subject, as when I was growing up you could guarantee that Irish television was not doing many programmes on issues such as depression, anxiety or teenage suicide.

I was due to speak on the show with Kathleen Lynch, the Minister of State at the Department of Health, who oversaw provision for mental health in her department, and with Professor Jim Lucey, the head of St Patrick's Mental Health Services, but I was reluctant to get pulled into a political or statistical analysis of the subject, so I was relieved when I was told a young man called 'Jack' would also speak of his own personal experiences. On the show, I spoke briefly and openly about my past and about why I felt it was important to increase awareness and bring attention to mental health. I was racked with nerves. I sometimes get slightly emotional when I speak of my experiences and I did not want to appear this way on a current affairs programme, especially with Miriam O'Callaghan, Ireland's flagship TV presenter who I had a lot of respect for, staring at me.

After I spoke, Miriam turned to Jack who was sitting in the audience, to ask him about his story. He was a man of 19, but much older than his years. The next two minutes were momentous, and the fact that it was broadcast to hundreds of thousands of television viewers across

Ireland made it all the more powerful. Jack told his story with a rawness and honesty that undoubtedly saved lives. He spoke to the camera of his suicide attempt and how empty he felt, how alone and how frightened he was. He appealed to teenagers to seek help and not to suffer in silence. The live audience in front of us were so touched as Jack fought off the tears, and it had an immense impact on me. I kept seeing myself in these stories. When you go through these issues you feel uniquely alone. No one on this planet knows how you are feeling but the reality is, millions upon millions of people know exactly how you are feeling. It may not be identical to their feeling, but at the core it's the same thing. As Jack finished with the words 'My life is better now than it ever has been, I am stronger than I ever have been,' I truly don't think he had any idea of the impact he was having on a country so scared off by issues such as these. In a society that still perceives mental illness as a weakness I can say one thing for sure: I don't know many men that would have the strength to do what Jack did that night.

12. So things can grow

AFTER MY *PRIME TIME* APPEARANCE I received a wave of goodwill and support that was truly remarkable. For years, I stubbornly believed we lived in a society that was ignorant and lacking education when it came to mental illness, but I started to see that it was not always ignorance or lack of understanding that stopped people engaging in conversation, it was fear. People were stopping me on the street to tell me their stories, men would approach me in pubs to say they were having a tough time, mothers and fathers would email me to say their son or daughter had watched *Prime Time* and opened up to them, while even friends of mine, people I thought I knew well, told me of the emotional and mental distress they disguised for years. It was a watershed.

I had also disguised so much from my friends over the years, so I was immediately able to relate to these silences they talked about, and when honesty is instilled into a relationship, bonds become stronger and you start to realise the true meaning of the word friendship. I remember one close friend of mine opening up about his struggles and watching his entire body collapse with relief, his shoulders fall as if a ten-ton weight had just been removed. He cried for almost an hour as he confided in me, and each tear seemed to release a repressed emotion that had choked and suffocated him all his life. We are a strange breed, us humans, that we allow ourselves deal with such pain, out of fear of how others will perceive and judge us. When my friend, a tough, talented and hugely impressive man, finally was able to admit to someone that he was not emotionally invincible, he was able to start taking back control of his life and seek recovery.

I very quickly realised that I was living in a country that for too long has expected people to act like robots, while in the vast majority of sectors within society, human emotions were placed far down the pecking order of importance. Only now with a clear head, where I feel strong and in control, can I look at this situation and observe how truly skewed, twisted and harmful it is. I want to help change it.

Over the following few months I spoke to thousands of people about their own struggles or the struggles of their loved ones. Mental illness does not just affect one person; the entire family has to deal with the pain. Mothers would tell me of their agony at not being able to comfort or help their child, how utterly useless they felt at times. I feel that families need much more support on this level as it can tear them apart, leave fissures in relationships. I recently heard a documentary on RTÉ Radio 1 about a family living with depression. It started with the mother of the house playing the piano while saying she only plays the piano when she feels content and happy, suggesting that she very rarely plays it anymore. It turned out that her husband had been living with clinical depression for a number of years. I listened to the podcast while walking into town one day, hearing the stories of the eldest son trying to comfort his father, while the daughter said she often felt scared when he was really low as he became aggressive. It was a heartbreaking 30 minutes that opened my eyes to the struggles faced by not only the person dealing with the illness, but their families and loved ones. It's easy to forget those collateral effects.

My acceptance of my condition coincided with a period of open and healthy public debate surrounding mental health. The mood in the country was of compassion, and I was showing some self-compassion. The element of anger, that repressive, fraught feeling in my stomach, was leaving me. Now it was time to set some goals and challenges. In July 2013 I found myself doing my first triathlon in Lanesborough in County Longford. Having done an open-water swim, narrowly avoiding an intimate experience with a seal, I was relatively calm at the idea of swimming in the River Shannon for the event. Though something that hadn't crossed my mind was that I would be entering the water with six or seven hundred other people at the same time.

A swim start in a triathlon is a frightening experience for anyone not versed in the phenomenon. Hundreds of people swimming over each other in deep water, getting kicked, punched and pushed under the surface, while the water ruptures like a banjaxed industrial washing machine. As I stood at the shore, looking out at the swim course, I felt that unwelcome sense of panic flow through my body. It was a day of tropical heat and because the river was next to a power plant the water was peaty, Guinness black, and altogether unknown beneath us. I found it difficult to swallow, while the pressure on my chest was indicating that perhaps an anxiety attack was around the corner. I was with my good friend Derry, who had said he would do the race to support me. He started to sense the turn in my mood.

In the past, if I found myself on the verge of a panic attack, I would make up some weak excuse as to why I could not do the activity I was facing, and disappear. This would get me out of the situation, but bury me inside as I knew I was letting not just myself down, but those trainers and friends who had invested the time in me to help me get to that point.

However, I remembered I was now a different person, armed with coping strategies used to deal with this very type of situation.

Leading up to the race I had discovered a simple technique that had its foundations in hypnotism and CBT, which I liked to call 'the magic moment technique'. For the weeks leading up to the triathlon, as I was falling asleep I would think of a situation in the past where I felt truly happy and content. I would always revert back to a childhood memory of my Granny Mac bringing me to a shop in Glasgow to buy me the full Celtic Football Club strip – jersey, shorts and socks – and think of how exciting it was. When the memory felt vivid in my head I would squeeze my thumb and forefinger together tightly on my right hand and hold it for a few minutes, breathing deeply. I practised this every night for three or four weeks with focused enthusiasm.

The idea behind the technique is that when you find yourself in situations that cause you panic, by squeezing your two fingers together, your subconscious will bring you to that place of calm and contentment, that magic moment.

Standing on the shore, I closed my eyes for a whole minute and squeezed my thumb and forefinger together. My heart rate lowered, the tension in my chest reduced and I found myself becoming focused and even excited about the new experience that lay ahead, knowing my internal resilience would guide me through my first triathlon. As the hundreds of swimmers entered the water before the start of the race, everyone looked extremely tense and nervous. Derry turned to me and said, 'Jesus,

Bressie, what has you so chilled out? I thought you hated water.' Not anymore, mate.

When the gun went off to mark the start of the race, I took off, embracing the full anarchy of something that only a few years previously would have seemed completely impossible. I smiled through that race, spitting out mouthfuls of salty peat water.

Myself and Derry crossed the finish line together and I will never forget the support and friendship he showed me that day. I drove back to Mullingar after the race with a sense of pride in myself that in the past was rarely evident. I had found the self-compassion that had eluded me for so long, and that evening I shared a pint or two with my father in our local, Davy Finn's, to congratulate myself.

I had the bug. Only four weeks later I found myself in the beautiful town of Kilkenny doing my second triathlon. I engaged with the same coping mechanisms to maintain my focus and reduce my pre-race anxiety and it worked incredibly well. I even found myself helping anyone nervous around me to remain calm in the water. Having spent years of my life believing I was mentally flawed, I was quickly discovering I was anything but; in fact, my biggest asset now was my mental strength and resilience. I only wish I had possessed these skills years before as a professional athlete. When I came over the finish line in Kilkenny, completely exhausted, my sister Laura passed me her baby son, Billy, to congratulate me. He hugged me tight and smiled at me, and it was a moment I will never forget till the day I die. A rush of emotion ran through me for that brief second, until he realised I stank and was covered in sweat and started bawling to get away from me. It was the fact I was able to experience these real moments of happiness that indicated I was well and truly on my way down the road of recovery. I love my nephew Billy so much, and it feels good to have this emotion so unchallenged. God help me when I have kids of my own, I will be like that cartoon character Elmyra in *Animaniacs*, a possessive young girl who used to hug her pets almost to death with love.

At this stage, endurance sport was really becoming a welcome release for me. Getting out on a bike for a few hours or a run offered me a calmness and comfort that many other things couldn't do. Later that summer, Roz and I went down to Tipperary to have a break and visit her parents. Feeling a little ambitious, I decided to go out on a cycle with the Carrick Wheelers, a renowned and respected cycling club in the region. That area is also the home of one of Ireland's most celebrated elite athletes, cyclist Sean Kelly. I was stunned to notice Sean had joined us for the cycle. About 30km into the spin I realised that I was way out of my league. I was desperately holding on to the back of the peloton, hunched forward and arms outstretched, looking like an extra from a zombie movie. I was so stubborn that I refused to drop back and do the honourable thing and admit that I was blowing out of my arse with exhaustion. They were going so fast that I couldn't even grab a sip of water or a bit of food and I could feel my legs turning to jelly and my head becoming dizzy as my blood sugar levels dropped dramatically.

But I hung on, because I was mad to chat to Sean Kelly, and pick his brains about his training and other stories of the races he had done over the years. I mustered up the last drop of energy left in my body and cycled up towards Sean, greeting him, while pretending that I was well able for the pace and there was not a bother on me. I burnt the ear off him for five or 10 minutes before dropping back to my rightful place at the very back of the peloton. I turned to one of the other cyclists in the group and I remember gingerly saying to him, 'Jaysus, Sean is some man, dead sound.' He looked at me blankly and with a tinge of sympathy politely informed me, 'Eh, that's not Sean Kelly, ye dope.' In my devastatingly fatigued state I managed to confuse one of Ireland's greatest ever athletes with some complete randomer who must have thought I was quite odd, as I quizzed him about the Tour de France and the Giro d'Italia. That was quite a lesson to learn. Curb the enthusiasm.

During the summer of 2013 I started to recognise quite a few things about myself. For years I allowed other people's attitudes to define and control my identity. I sometimes found myself doing things to please others rather than myself, and I sacrificed my values accordingly. I began to discover that without values we become the robots society expects us to be. I asked myself over those months, what do I actually stand for? Regaining your sense of identity is a core building block to recovery and it can take some tough decisions to ultimately achieve that.

I started to ask myself, having been a solo artist for a few years now, was I really enjoying it? I loved my band, they were top-notch guys, but inside, I found, I really did not get anything out of being a solo artist. I was making music that I had no personal attachment to. I was sacrificing the creative values Michael Beinhorn had taught me for commercial values driven by the market. I missed the rough and ready environment of playing with The Blizzards. That unbeatable buzz of being creative with other musicians. I was getting great support as a solo artist and it was going relatively well but deep down I was not happy.

That August I spoke with my manager, Dougie, and told him I was going to retire as a solo artist. He was incredibly understanding. The hunger was gone. Plus, retiring was of course my forte. I put together a press release and only a few days later I was no longer a solo artist. I am extremely grateful for all the support I received, but I needed to make the decision for myself; after all, I've sung the words before: 'You can't stay young forever'. Ok, I'll get my jacket … taxi.

My good friend from Mullingar and mental health campaigner Marty Mulligan called me a week later to put an idea to me. He was the director of the Spoken

Word stage in the Mindfield area at Electric Picnic, one of Ireland's most popular music and culture festivals. Marty wanted to know would I speak on the stage about my journey through mental health. That was kind of strange. I had for years played at festivals and now I was being asked to speak at one. I had my reservations. I had visions of walking onto a stage to speak with a tent full of pissed punters wanting to have a bit of craic for the weekend. The last thing they needed was me getting up and speaking about panic attacks and depression. Marty assured me that the audience would be respectful and engaging with the topic so I took his word for it. I stood at the side of the stage with Jim Breen as Marty introduced us. What happened next was unforgettable. Marty, a world-class slam poet, told the crowd that he lives with his own mental health issues. As he recited one of the most moving and personal two minutes of slam poetry I had ever heard, titled 'This Will Pass', a line jumped out at me. 'Don't see rain as depressing, see it as earth's blessing, so things can grow'.

It was almost my turn to speak. Once again at the side of the stage I found myself practising my relaxation techniques, and the more I practised them, the more they benefited and supported me when I required them.

I got up and told my story with a raw honesty that surprised even me. Though I was always incredibly open about my past, here, I found myself saying things I have never said out loud. The reaction from the audience was warm and uplifting; there wasn't the negative and buzz-wrecking atmosphere I had expected, but one of positivity, hope and celebration. Here we were at a festival, on a stage, talking openly about our emotions and it was completely liberating on all fronts. It felt like this was the start of some kind of movement, a movement that would filter out across the country and help spread the message so many amazing awareness groups and charities have been spreading for years, that 'It's okay not to feel okay, and it's absolutely okay to ask for help.'

I was confident I had something to offer teenagers, who I felt might benefit most from a discussion about mental health yet who can be the hardest to reach. I had an idea for an effective way to reach out to them. During the coming weeks, I commenced work on producing an album for the Cycle Against Suicide. I put a call out to a few of my friends in the industry asking them would they get involved with the project aimed at creating awareness among their fan base. Some of the biggest bands and artists in the country got on board straight away, contributing a song written specifically for the album which was titled *Simple Things* after the title track, a stunning song written by Michael Kavanagh. The vast majority of artists involved had a strong teenage following, and when a teenager sees their idols or heroes speak or sing about mental health, it helps to normalise them, and it helps them recognise that they are not alone. That for me is why this record was so important, it communicated with teenagers, often the very people who find it most difficult to deal with their mental health. The whole theme of the record was aimed at promoting help-seeking behaviour and I have no doubt these songs had an important influence on many teenagers across this country.

The next thing was to record it, a thorny and exhausting process, I quickly remembered. There were 12 different acts, 12 different songs, 12 different creative impulses packed into this album. We commissioned inspiring young artists like The Coronas, Heathers, Gavin James and Ryan Sheridan, to name but a few. I wanted the sound to be relaxed and personable so a teenager could put their headphones on and immediately connect with it as if they were in the room with the artist, almost as Tom Waits' *Closing Time* had done for me. Achieving this meant caution was thrown to the wind. I was locking horns with peers to get it right, holed up in the studio almost 24/7 for five days, eating the worst kind of foods – Hobnobs and Jaffa Cakes all day and then takeaways – and petrol station red wine from a plastic cup to relax myself so I could sleep. In the night, my head would race with the minutiae of producing the songs and I emerged from the process fatigued and run down. I noticed my mood lowering dramatically. I became very dismissive and short with Roz, and gave her no time. I found it hard to motivate myself or even get out of bed.

Myself and Jeffrey had been getting on so well lately that this was an unexpected and unwelcome recommencement of hostilities between us. This time, instead of allowing myself to get frustrated or upset I allowed this cloud of depression to sweep over me, constantly repeating Marty Mulligan's refrain that 'This will pass'. I did not try to be positive, I did not try relaxation techniques. I just let it sweep over me, knowing in the back of my mind that in a day or two I would be fine. This approach works for me. I am totally aware that although I have come a long way with my mental health, there will be days when I get low or deeply anxious, just like there will be days when I get bugs and infections. I now treat my mental health the way I treat my physical health: some days you just feel shit.

I looked back at what could have brought on the mood swing after the recording process. I started going over the list of Jeffrey's likes and dislikes and it became instantly evident why I ended up feeling this way. Producing the *Simple Things* album, I had run my immune system into the ground, eating the worst of foods and courting stress, and it had retaliated accordingly. Now when I go into a studio I bring my own snacks and healthy dinners, I don't drink alcohol and I only allow myself to track for a maximum of eight hours a day. I exercise before I arrive into the studio and if the shit hits the fan while recording I have to fall back on my coping mechanisms, and they don't fail me.

Being able to stand back and recognise the effects of certain actions on your state of mind is a fundamental resource for people who seek recovery. Sometimes these actions are enjoyable at the time but then they bite back afterwards, so you really have to do a cost – benefit analysis to highlight which actions need to be curtailed and which actions need to be promoted. When you are drinking wine at the end of a recording session, naturally, after a few glasses, everything sounds amazing. When you come back in the morning, you don't only end up having a hangover, the mix sounds pretty crap as well. Alcohol is not good for the honing of a sharp objective ear.

One miserably wet and cold evening in October 2013 I was driving home to see my parents, listening to *Off the Ball* on Newstalk. There was an interview with an ex-Cork hurler, Conor Cusack, about a recent blog he had written on his experiences with depression. I had to pull the car in off the N4 as he gave his account of the illness. I had never heard anyone speak the way he did about the subject. Perhaps it was his commanding and gladiatorial Cork speech, but the language he used was so full of imagery, yet so accurate and emotional. He spoke of one evening waiting for his parents to go to mass so he could take his own life. I could not believe what I was hearing on the radio. Here was a high-performance inter-country athlete, playing one of the world's toughest sports, speaking of this crippling mental illness. As tough as the interview was to listen to, I was so excited by the fact that such an influential communicator like Conor was coming forward to help break the stigma in this country around mental health. When I got home I jumped straight onto the internet to look at this blog he had written. I must have read it ten times, and each time I read it, it became more and more commanding. I found Conor on Twitter and let him know how incredible this piece of writing was. His response was 'Thank you for your kind words, *a chara.*' It became clear to me quite quickly that this man was going to have a seriously positive impact on the people of Ireland and beyond.

13. Business and pleasure

SOMETHING WAS BECOMING UNDENIABLY EVIDENT in the discussion around mental health throughout all sectors of society. Even elderly men and women who had experienced a much more historically prejudicial stigma, that had been compressed throughout generations of silence and shame, were speaking up about the emotional issues they had to face, even without the support of friends and family who couldn't comprehend their illness. Professional and elite athletes, often perceived as invincible superhumans with a commanding physical and mental strength, were discussing how they, at times, faced a darkness that robbed them of all their power. Teenagers and their teachers were running mental health awareness weeks, where only a year earlier, the Cycle Against Suicide organisers were struggling for access into schools to discuss mental health and emotional wellbeing. Companies were slowly beginning to recognise that investing in the wellness of their employees could have both economic and social benefits, once they stopped treating their staff like robots.

Following one corporate wellness presentation I gave, I got talking to a partner in a legal firm about the need for organisations to value the wellness of their employees and must say I was left slightly appalled. This man told me that he worked long hours and sacrificed so much to get to where he got to, and it didn't do him any harm, so why is it an issue? I asked him what his relationship with his children and wife was like. He said he was divorced and had a civil but hands-off relationship with his sons, who he felt awkward talking to. So yes, he may be hugely successful as a businessman, with a very healthy bank balance, but he had no relationship with his kids and seemed to lack emotional intelligence. I know what I would rather have if I had the choice, but when money and status consistently come ahead of humanity and emotional wellbeing, perhaps it's harder to see the wood from the trees in terms of what really matters.

There was a direct correlation between the increased discourse around mental health and the prime-time media attention it was receiving. In general, prime-time media slots have tended to veer away from the discussion, due to the perceived heaviness of the topic, which unfortunately leads to a head-in-the-sand approach, bolstering the already stubborn stigma.

I was grateful to have caught this wave of public concern. As I saw I could have some role to play in the future, I focused on becoming a more effective communicator, finding ways to convey the passion I felt. It was a long way from the monosyllabic, socially inept teenager who first graced these pages. With the release of the *Simple Things* record, myself and Alan O'Mara, a footballer with Cavan and one of the ambassadors for the Cycle Against Suicide, were invited onto one of RTÉ's biggest entertainment and lifestyle shows, *The Saturday Night Show*. I had spoken on the subject on current affairs shows, but this was reaching an entirely different audience. Myself and a handful of artists performed the title track from *Simple Things* before I made my way over to the host, Brendan O'Connor, to be interviewed alongside Alan.

The minute I sat down, I began to sweat from both my face and arms. This is a nervous reaction I sometimes experience but I had not felt any nerves up until that point. It's one of those great psychological debates, does the physiological reaction cause the psychological reaction, or vice-versa? I thought I had that one figured so this was new to me, profuse sweating without the attendant panic. Jeffrey, don't be a dick, I thought to myself. I became so concerned about what might happen next that the sweat started dripping from my face, which of course just made me sweat more. I had half a can of Lynx on under my arms and the perspiration still continued to stream down my back. I was finding it hard to focus on Brendan's very probing questions and I knew I looked nervous. I could not practise my coping techniques as I did not want to be sitting there with my eyes closed, breathing deeply while Brendan was chatting to me about depression and anxiety. It wouldn't have been a good look for mental health awareness.

I felt the flutter of panic as I missed a breath while Alan was being questioned about his own struggle with depression. I reached for a glass of water, to occupy my head with an action, while I searched for an appropriate coping strategy that could get me through the coming minutes. So many people have spoken to me about the crippling social anxiety they face when asked to speak in public. My first question is 'What are you doing about it?' 'Oh, I just picture the crowd naked' is a common answer. Whichever genius philosopher came up with that theory needs a kick in the shins. I really do not think me picturing *The Saturday Night Show* audience in the nip was going to help me out of the hole I found myself in that evening. The only way was to use the weapons I had been given when I searched for a treatment to my condition.

As my anxiety grew, I refused to let myself lose control, and implemented a technique I had acquired through my education in CBT. I attempted to remove myself mentally from my own body and look at myself, my actions and my behaviours, as if through someone else's eyes. Once I could look at myself objectively I realised that I was thinking irrationally. To all the audience, I must have looked like a normal and quite relaxed bloke; I was smiling, legs crossed, arm across the sofa. The thought of this immediately calmed my heart rate and allowed me to regain composure while Alan was speaking, and when it was my turn to be asked a question, I was focused and concise with my answers.

Brendan O'Connor was very respectful of and interested in the subject of mental health, and the interview flowed. After the show ended, I was extremely thankful that I had an arsenal of coping mechanisms I could rely on in these inevitable times of anxiety. I felt almost bulletproof. I can't tell you how much a situation like that would have torn me in two in the past, and how I would simply not have been able to cope, but thanks to my close and understanding relationship with Jeffrey, I was able to regain control. Apart from the fact that my shirt was soaked straight through with the sweat, I appeared relatively normal. I made my way back to my dressing room just to gather myself and change. I needed that brief few minutes to allow myself space before joining friends in the green room, but suddenly my phone was vibrating with texts and tweets and calls. Although I had spoken publicly about my anxiety and depression, there were still plenty of people completely unaware of it. People I knew from school, people I went to college with, people I worked with or played rugby with.

I couldn't help but open my phone. As I scrolled through the tweets, then the texts, every hair on the back of my neck stood up, every cell in my body was overwhelmed with a sincere emotion, not of sadness but of happiness. Half a million people were watching this at home, and an entirely different audience to that which I had reached before. Perhaps some of them turned to their loved ones, right there and then, to ask for help. Friends I went to school with thanked me because they were finally able to tell their parents or partner; families destroyed by depression and silenced by the stigma told me how relieved they were now that it was being spoken about on talk shows in Ireland. Every time in the past I had performed or spoken on a show such as this you could guarantee a small element of abuse on social media, the usual shite, but the response on this night was one hundred per cent positive and supportive.

People often tell me that the biggest obstacle preventing them from seeking help is how they believe they will be treated by others. Will they get abused online or looked at sidelong on the street if someone finds out they have a problem with their mental health? It's hard for me to say anything to support them, so all I can do is outline my experience of seeking help, which in the end was profoundly positive. People are ready to talk now, they want to talk and they want to engage with others who may be experiencing what they experience, who may be able to support and offer advice on certain treatments and therapies. The reality is, in most primary cases, issues with mental health are treatable. What is stopping people seeking that treatment is an ignorant and pointless stigma. Think of it this way: if we were to put physical and mental illnesses on the same page, could you imagine being diagnosed with cancer and being scared of seeking help, or even unable to receive help? We need to try and look at mental health in the same way. People unable to get support or too frightened to seek help are needlessly taking their own lives up and down our country. I believe now is the right time to push and make changes to how we perceive mental health. There is a real hunger for evolution in our attitudes towards mental health, let's not throw this opportunity away. The difficulty for some people is that when they get past that stigma, they are confronted with the new obstacle course of finding adequate services.

At Christmas 2013 I decided to set myself a challenge that would involve a big commitment, both time-wise and head-wise. Having enjoyed how triathlons pulled me from my comfort zone, I decided to take on a bigger challenge in an ironman 70.3 triathlon, which consisted of a 2km swim, 90km cycle and a half marathon, all done consecutively. Despite having taken positive strides with my mental health, I still wasn't sleeping well at all. I knew that in order to stay on top of my anxiety and depression I had to continuously find new challenges that pushed me, but more importantly focused me on specific goals. Jeffrey liked having that mental structure that allowed him to aim at certain targets while at the same time prevented him from steering off course and thinking about other things, things that were out of his and my control.

I know it can come across as a touch self-righteous, this triathlon culture. Imposing momentous challenges on ourselves and getting absorbed in training for months in advance seems like a strange club to be part of. Sometimes when training, getting out on a bike in the dawn frost you'd wonder to yourself, what am I actually doing here? Chill out, it's Christmas. But these goals have been very important in my story. They meant regaining control of a life that I had let run away from myself. Pushing my body and mind to its absolute limit, and then going beyond that limit, became a form of medication. It is very rewarding to find strength of body and mind in yourself, when you know what weakness and hopelessness feel like.

I signed up to the 70.3 ironman in St Polten in Austria in May 2014. Not sure why I chose Austria, maybe it was because of my subconscious love of *The Sound of Music*, but either way, there was no going back. Myself and Roz decided to go away to La Santa, a triathlon training camp in Lanzarote for Christmas which was the first time in my life I would be away from my family during the festive period. Over the previous years I had spent my Christmases getting drunk, eating industrial tins of Quality Street and hoping that my head would be good to me, and now I found myself swimming, riding bikes and running while swapping the Guinness and whiskey for beetroot juices and wheatgrass shots. Even writing this I want to punch myself in the face, as it comes across as sickeningly self-righteous, but the disparity between abusing alcohol and using exercise is so vast, I soaked up every minute of the preparations.

I always find it hard to sleep when I go away anywhere, whether it's for work or for a holiday. I can toss and turn for hours if I am not used to the environment. Plenty of people are like this but I am the type that can let it get to me, and this can often become debilitating, and more often than not, results in me requiring alcohol to get to sleep, or worse, self-medicating. Frustrated by sleep deprivation, I was sometimes not afraid to drink until alcohol had a comatose effect. In Lanzarote, that really was not going to be an option when you had to get up the next morning and ride your bike for five hours in the hot sun. So I got my hands on some sleeping pills, my old enemy.

This addiction is the thing I was most ashamed of all my life. I had been to my GP Doctor Healy not long before, and come clean about my habit. 'How many are you talking about, two or three a week?' he asked me. 'More like two or three a night,' I said, and his face went white. He knew about the serious mental health and liver damage risks that prolonged use of these drugs cause. We had a serious conversation about this, and he gave me a programme to take me down off my addiction. But I still slipped some in my bag in case I could not sleep at all while in Lanzarote. I knew that no matter how anxious I felt while away, they would take care of that. My first mistake was the amount I ended up bringing. I had a box of 24 and I knew that I could easily end up going through them. I hid them from Roz, which really wasn't fair, because she wasn't comfortable with my taking sleeping pills without a prescription. When she found the box next to my bag I promised her that I had brought them along 'just in case', and that I would not need to take them.

The first night we arrived I took a pill and it knocked me out clean. I woke up the following morning and was barely able to get out of my bed I was so wrecked. I then proceeded to take a couple of pills every night, behind Roz's back. I hated myself for it and felt a profound guilt that I had allowed myself to fall back into this really unhealthy habit, and also that I was lying to my girlfriend, someone I was always so honest with. Though when you wake up in the morning with cotton mouth because you're so dehydrated by these pills, you can't keep up the lie.

On 25 December, instead of having Christmas dinner we went to a local resort restaurant for steak and chips. This is how, almost by way of some devilish karma, I found myself contracting an ungodly bout of food poisoning. On the car ride back to our hotel I could feel the cramps starting in my stomach. By the time we got home I was violently ill, and had to camp in our toilet for the night, vomiting among other things every couple of minutes. Whatever girlfriend/boyfriend awkwardness that existed between myself and Roz was well and truly eradicated that night, and over the coming days. Before you knew it, Roz was going through the same thing. We were all over the place. I would take a sleeping pill to try and sleep it off but vomit it straight back up only a few minutes later. In my depleted state I felt convinced this was some kind of punishment for slipping back into my old ways.

As I started to come through and was able to leave the bathroom for longer than five minutes without fear of sacrificing what little integrity I had left, I had a pretty stern chat with Jeffrey. I was not going to dwell on this minor misfortune, not going to let this rough couple of days set me back. I flushed the remaining pills down the slightly distressed toilet and to this day I have never engaged with sleeping pills again, and have absolutely no intention of doing so in the future.

Recovery, for me, is an ongoing process. There will be periods when it does not go so well, and there will be periods when you feel in complete control, and to be fair, these periods have become much more frequent the more I learned about myself and Jeffrey. Rather than beat myself up about the knockbacks, I chose to be proud of what I had already achieved and what I was aiming to achieve. I showed gratitude for the fact that we had got better and were able to go out cycling and running, embracing the sun and the relaxed atmosphere of the island. This allowed me to put this bump behind me but it also reminded me of how important it is to be aware of myself and the need to constantly work on my mental fitness and coping techniques.

Myself and Roz flew home from our excursion before the New Year. Our plane was diverted to land in Shannon Airport due to one of the worst storms Ireland had seen in years. All the relaxation techniques I had learned went out the window as our Aer Lingus plane was thrown around the sky like a leaf in a gust of wind. Even the air stewards had that 'Fuck, we are going to die' expression on their faces. I was in some state of fear.

Luckily we survived, but the next day we had signed up for a mental strength immersion camp weekend up in the stunning landscape of Delphi in Connemara, which was run by Gerry Hussey, my friend and mentor. Gerry said it would be quite a relaxed affair, concentrating more on the mental development of elite athletes. Relaxed me arse. He dragged us out of bed at 6am the following morning in the middle of the storm to climb a mountain while lugging a ten-stone log of wood among us. Roz and I still had no appetite, we were as pale as death before going up that hill. I was raging and wanted to throw Gerry off the top of the mountain but there was a method to his madness; after all, he's a professional.

We climbed back down, exhausted and courting hypothermia, and attempted a breakfast before Gerry informed us of a workshop we would do during the morning.

Gerry took the workshop with Alan Kerins, the Galway GAA legend and all-round top-class bloke. When I get fatigued or just plain exhausted, I tend to get slightly more emotional and open up more, and this by all accounts is a common trait. It was Gerry's plan, to get us bollixed tired then make us cry. Evil genius.

That morning we sat around a table with a handful of elite athletes, in a warm room in Delphi by a stone fire. We could see snow-peaked mountains and glaciated valleys carved into a spectacular landscape around us. Once we had collected ourselves, Gerry asked the group something I don't think I had ever been asked before. He said, 'What do you stand for, what are your values? Without values you have nothing.'

The question mesmerised me. In truth, even though I had been reflecting on it for some time, I wasn't sure I had the answer, and I am not quite sure any of us can answer this so simply. In a world so clouded by distractions and chaos we rarely get to stand back and ask ourselves this question, yet values are the very thing that define and motivate us. During that two-hour workshop I started to realise that I needed to establish my values and live by them, and not allow anyone define, construct or destruct my values for me. That morning planted a seed in me, it was an invitation to go and find out my values, which is at the core of what now drives me. I knew walking out of that workshop that I wanted to help others realise the importance of establishing theirs too.

The continued public discourse around the subject of emotional wellbeing and mental health did not slow down going into the New Year. The New Year is a strange time for many people and it often involves new beginnings but it can also be an incredibly difficult period for people who experience bouts of depression. There can be a sting to our finances, while the body might be tender after the overindulgent festive season. The weather is dark, wet and cold and the world can generally seem lethargic and uninspiring. It's important for people who experience this seasonal low to look at ways to limit its effect. In my case I was lucky, as I had the ironman training to keep me focused and goal-orientated but there were certainly nights when I felt completely out of sorts and very down. This is totally normal and totally manageable, I reminded myself.

People tend to make sweeping and often sudden changes to their lifestyle in the New Year with all the resolution messing that goes on. Something that Gerry Hussey taught me in the immersion camp in Delphi was that in finding your values, you will find your motivations. People might decide that they want to go to the gym every day and stay away from sugar and alcohol, but they fail to ask themselves, why? Is it to lose weight and feel better about themselves, or to lose weight and look better? All motivations have a deeper core to them and can be traced back to a person's values, to what we stand for. I often hear people say during the New Year after breaking their resolutions that they have no willpower, as if willpower is some rare personality trait that they have not been innately blessed with. A person's willpower is a sister to their motivations, which in turn is related to their values. Now at the risk of sounding like Oprah Winfrey, it's entirely up to the individual to define their values and hence their motivations. Waiting to be spoon-fed what we should value is not an advisable life strategy. Being able to establish this ourselves can really support an individual's recovery and aid them on their way to taking back control of their lives.

A few weeks into the New Year, the Cycle Against Suicide, by now inundated with requests from schools to visit them, decided to host a leaders' congress exhibition in the RDS in Dublin, where over 5,000 teenagers attended the events from all around Ireland. Now that is progress. Teachers up and down the country brought their students to help raise their awareness about mental health in this country. Myself and others like Conor Cusack and Munster and Ireland rugby player Alan Quinlan addressed the students and described our journey. The day was a massive indication of how far we have travelled in this country on this topic and how committed our students and schools are to learning about the mind. During one of the speeches I noticed a young teenage lad sitting at the side of the stage, and while I should have been concentrating on the talk, something about him worried me.

He was sitting with his shoulders stooped, clutching his arms and his eyes were glazed, fixed downwards to the floor. To others it looked as if he was just emotional but to me it was clear he was in the infancy of a panic attack. I've got a sixth sense for a panic attack. I've been there so many times I have become hypersensitive to its physical signs, so I made my way towards him, careful not to freak him out. He looked up, and I could see a tear running down the face of this young lad. He now had his hand on his chest and I could see his breath become shallower as the tears began to flow more freely from his eyes. I had to reach out. I know there is nothing anyone can say or do to stop it once it's started or make it any easier but I just wanted him to know it was normal.

When I got to him, I greeted him, and put my hand gently on his shoulder. He was in the depths of panic at this stage and was trying desperately to catch a breath. I held his stare and told him that this would be over in a minute. He barely looked at me, he was shaking now. Watching someone go through this, it brings back frightening memories of my own, but I hoped maybe I could help him. His eyes were glazed over as if I didn't exist, until I said to him, 'Have a bite of an apple.' He looked at me with that 'What kind of gobshite are you?' look I've been given many times in my life, but as his concentration veturned to my stupid suggestion he briefly forgot he was having a panic attack and seemed to calm down. He forgot to even ask about the apple, luckily, because I didn't have one. It was something that had worked for me in the past, to think or say the most leftfield thing you can come up with and it sometimes tricks someone back into the present moment.

As this teenager slowly calmed down he became very tearful, so the organisers and I took him backstage. He kept crying and asking me why he had to live with it. I didn't have any answers. After all, a person's mental health is unique to themselves, but I kept telling him how normal this is, how I lived with this all my life and that one day he'll find a way of coping with panic attacks and even using them to motivate and drive him. I explained to him what exactly a panic attack is and was shocked to realise that although he had been experiencing them for three years, he had never sought help; no one had ever told him why they can happen and how to try to cope with them. He calmed down, seeming to have a clearer grasp of this condition. It concerned me that this had never been brought up in his school or that students were not being educated on something quite common but deeply distressing for those experiencing it. There is abundant information available on the internet but it is scattered and, and knowledge should come from an adult or a peer and not from a Google search.

I believe mental health awareness weeks are fantastic

for schools, and something we should very much celebrate, but the thing about emotional wellbeing is that it takes practice. It's like any sport, or creative art, or learning how to drive, or fitness training. It all takes practice, and until we start to engage our teenagers and kids in daily practice, we won't really notice any long-term generational improvements in their mental health. Awareness, as I said, is brilliant, but we need to start implementing ways of making our teenagers and kids mentally fitter, so that they can cope with all the traumas and stresses life throws at them. We must build resilience among all our teenagers and kids, not just the ones experiencing problems but each and every one of them. Only then will we notice the cultural evolution around the subject. Teaching and helping just the 20 per cent or so of people with issues and ignoring the 80 per cent without issues is not a sustainable solution. All our youth must be equipped and supported on all fronts. The education system must invest massively in school counsellors, not just for the students but for the teachers. They need emotional support and guidance too and it's paramount that we look after their needs. No one is asking teachers to become therapists, that's not their job, but I feel if they integrated some mindfulness and awareness periods into their class it could prove beyond beneficial. The teachers in my school had no problem saying prayers at the start of every lesson so why can't we offer up three or four minutes a day to practise and outline mindfulness techniques?

Over the following months I threw myself into my training, setting out a strict daily routine. I started working on a new documentary called *Teenage Kicks*, shot in one of my favourite cities in Ireland, Limerick. I wanted to engage with the teenagers in that colourful place and explore the issues they face while using a common bond, our love of music. I worked with an incredibly special group of teenagers from some of the more disadvantaged areas of the city with an aim of making a record, starting a label and doing a gig. I grew very close to the band and we developed a huge element of trust and mutual respect for each other. They were happy to sit down and tell me their problems and the issues they faced and it made me realise that although they live in a different environment and different era to what I grew up in, their issues still affected them in exactly the same way. Pain is pain, and sadness is sadness. What they achieved in the months of filming will I hope stand to them for the rest of their lives. One of the biggest lessons it taught me was that if you empower a teenager they can do great things.

Too much of our language around teenagers is negative and unsupportive. Think of the unflattering moniker 'Generation Anxiety' often used in the national media to describe teenagers. Kids, regardless of their backgrounds, need to have self-worth, they need to be empowered and the widening gap that seems to be appearing between adults and teenagers needs to be tightened. Something else it taught me was that we can't look at everything in black and white. We can't assume that because a teenager does something bad that they are ill-disciplined. It's important to look further and search for the reasons behind their behaviour and then we can start looking at ways of improving that behaviour. I am not a psychologist or a doctor, but if you actually spend time with teenagers and learn to understand their world, you really get a picture of how they think. The 'Sure I went through that and I turned out grand' line is a load of bull and must be scrapped. The world teenagers are living in now compared to my generation may as well be in a different solar system. Let's stop isolating our teenagers and reconnect with them and try to understand the dynamic, progressive and often hostile world they live in.

As you might have guessed, I had some fairly urgent messages I wanted to impart at this time. It's one thing having a message, it's another matter finding the right way to communicate it, so I was coached by professionals on the finer details of public speaking. Eye contact, hand movements, when to take a long pause. I was often telling my own story, and without learning some techniques, I ran the risk of allowing myself to become over-emotional, losing my audience and leaving myself in ribbons. During 2014 I was invited to speak to major corporate businesses about their wellness programmes and work/life balance, stress and other issues in the workplace. I thought it was hilarious because the only company I ever worked in, I only lasted a few weeks. But it was clear that companies were recognising the need to look after the welfare of their employees, beyond free gym membership and drink-soaked Christmas parties.

When I stood in front of the staff to tell my story I was able to spot the people that were struggling in an instant. Of all the places I had spoken in before, it was clear the corporate environment was a ticking time bomb. There were still serious ripples from the recession, so many of the people I addressed must have been in a state of anxiety and stress over work security and finances. I had read in the news about people losing homes, and about relationships breaking down due to the added pressures of the faltering economy. I always insisted that there should be confidential counselling available to anyone that required it after a talk, but I knew that it was the top board of management that would ultimately make the call to change the culture within the workplace. Some managers engaged with me, while others did not see it as their job, nor the responsibility of the company. They could not have been more wrong. Employees define a business, and if they are unhappy their productivity will drop, which in turn will affect others, and eventually profits. Now I am no Michael O'Leary but I'll volunteer some advice to CEOs: there is a serious benefit to investment in employee emotional welfare.

The macho culture that exists in certain industries can be quite a road block for changing attitudes. I once gave a talk in a well-known bank and there were a hundred people in the crowd, ninety-four women and six men, I was told afterwards. What more is there to say about men's throwaway attitude to their emotional wellbeing? Not one of us who has been through the Irish recession and its colourful aftermath is unaware of the machismo of the banking culture. From what I can gather, the corporate culture has improved dramatically since the recession knockbacks. Although some companies are just ticking boxes when it comes to human resources, others are implementing programmes aimed at emotional support for their employees. It will take time but there certainly seems to be more willingness among the corporate world, and this has to be driven from the top down.

In the midst of all this I was still a coach on *The Voice of Ireland* and was lucky enough to see my very talented act Brendan McCahey win the show that April. Once the final was over, my entire focus shifted towards my first 70.3 ironman event, and time was quickly closing in on me. In just four weeks I would be travelling to Austria to attempt my first race and I had a lot of work to do. Physically I felt strong, and was probably as fit as I had ever been, but I wanted to actively work on my mental preparation for the race, which was quite difficult considering I had never done one, and hence I could not fully visualise the process. I started to watch ironman triathlons on YouTube to get a grasp of the more technical aspects of the event, and sought guidance from anyone willing to give it. Each evening I would pick a certain aspect of the race, such as the swim, and visualise myself going through my warm-ups and entering the water, getting into the rhythm of the stroke and leaving the water for the bike leg of the race. I would focus on one area that needed to work, such as my breathing, and picture myself calm and relaxed in the water.

Another technique I implemented came from an interview I heard with the world ironman champion, Chris McCormack. He said he would create mental folders in his head, as if he had them on a desktop, and each evening leading up to the event he would put positive phrases and words into a folder – words like 'power', 'focus', 'strength', 'champion' and leader' – and when he encountered a tough period of the race he would mentally drag those words out of the folder and onto his mental desktop. It was a very simple technique but it's often the simple ones, once practised, that can have the most positive effect. Every evening before I fell asleep, I would mentally open a folder and place words into it, which really gave me confidence. It reduced my pre-race anxiety and as the race got closer, I felt more and more excited and mentally prepared. Where once adrenaline rushed aimlessly through my veins, it was now like the fuel that was driving me.

Having objectified and humanised my issues in order to help me deal with my anxiety and depression, I was now chatting to Jeffrey as a friend who would help and support me through the 70.3 ironman. It was strangely comforting being able to say, 'Jeffrey, let's bloody nail this thing.' It kind of felt like he had my back.

I was remarkably calm in the week leading up to travelling to Austria. Roz was doing the race as well, but in her role as ambassador for the World Vision charity she had to travel to Jordan to visit refugee camps where displaced Syrians lived since the war began, and raise awareness. A noble thing to do, and certainly not the ideal preparation for the 70.3 ironman. She arrived back late on the Thursday evening emotionally and physically run-down, and we were flying out to Vienna early the next morning, before the race on Sunday. I felt for her as she had put so much work into her training over the winter and she did not really get to rest her body the way she should have before an endurance event such as this. Because I had put so much emphasis on my mental preparation, I was focused and very much ready for the race so I did my best to make the situation easier for Roz. I packed her bags for her and reassured her.

On the flight over I took some time to myself to visualise the race once again in my head. I love flying, it allows us to escape the world for a few hours and go on airplane mode, which is why I am not the biggest fan of the introduction of wireless internet onto planes. Why not just give our minds a few hours off? The internet will survive without us. After landing we travelled straight to St Polten, about two hours from Vienna, to register for the race and get our race numbers and packs. Seeing the buzz at the start area unleashed an energy within me that I had not felt in quite some time. Physically, I felt slightly out of place with all these elite athletes walking around, lean as a butcher's dog, but mentally I knew I was as strong as anyone else doing this race, so I soaked up the atmosphere and experience. I hadn't anticipated the heat. For some reason I assumed the weather in Austria was similar to Ireland but it was a lot warmer than I thought, especially when you are spending six hours out under the sun pushing your body to its limit.

The day before the race we decided to do the swim course just to get our bearings in the open water as it can be quite difficult to see where you are going when there are hundreds of other people splashing around next to you. Another technique I use when swimming to keep myself calm and focused on my stroke is to pick a song and sing it over and over in my head. It takes me away from the madness of a triathlon swim but still allows me concentrate enough on what I need to do. On this occasion I chose the nineties dance track 'Sunchyme' by Dario G, which was strange because I never liked that tune very much.

Once I got in for my practice swim I became almost too relaxed; what a strange departure from my phobia-stricken past. I felt incredibly at ease in the water and allowed myself to enjoy the process. Roz had a bit of a tough time in the practice swim and got upset, almost pulling out of the race, but I knew she was tough as nails and I just had to bring her back into the water to swim a little more and she was fine. There was no doubt she was quite exhausted from her week in Jordan. We went back to the hotel and tried to relax before the race the following day. In my head I kept reverting back to something Gerry Hussey had taught me: he said to 'embrace the chaos', and it made so much more sense to me now I was about to attempt a 70.3 ironman.

The evening before the race I spent an hour practising positive psychology techniques, showing gratitude, being mindful while another mentor of mine's advice ran through my head. Gerry Duffy, a fellow Mullingar man, and quite simply one of the most inspiring individuals I have ever had the good fortune to know, used to say to me, 'Remember, Niall, we get to do this.' Such a simple expression, it had so much influence on me that evening. Embrace the nerves and madness, let them fuel you but remember to be thankful that you are in a position to do an event like this. I managed to get myself into such a place of calm and happiness that evening that I really did not want the day to end.

We went to bed early as our call time the next morning was 5am, and my race started at 7am. The sun was rising as I woke up and just watching it slowly break the horizon gave me lashings of positive energy. I took a moment to appreciate how incredible it looked. I had slept straight through the night and was buzzing to get to the start line and soak up the atmosphere.

Even though it was my first time doing an event like this, it felt like I had done countless others as I had visualised each step of the process and prepared myself both mentally and physically to the best of my ability. Something else I knew I had was a deep and powerful resilience in difficult situations, but I hoped I would not need to call on this, to come head on with my own difficult situation – Jeffrey. After all, the work was done and I was ready for whatever was presented.

This was so much more than a race to me. This entire day represented how far I had come in my recovery, and I could not help but feel emotional. I did not want to let my emotions take over as I still had to focus on the specifics of the race, but inside I was so proud of myself for taking back control of my life and recognising that Jeffrey was not an enemy, just another part of me that needed to be appreciated and understood.

The women were going off in a separate wave so Roz got into the water ahead of me. I was so nervous for her, even though I was calm about my own race. As she stepped into the lake she went to tighten her goggles and the strap snapped. My heart sank, as once she entered the water she could not be helped. Her race was over before it started; all that training, all that commitment. But what did Roz do? She went on her back and did the back stroke, proving the incredible mental resources she has.

While I made my way into the water I was excited and chatting to everyone around me. Most of the other competitors were so nervous they didn't want their ear burnt off by a lanky Irish dude, plus very few of them spoke English. I felt a tap on my shoulder and when I turned around, a young man quietly said to me, 'It's a long way from *The Voice*.' Thank God, I thought, another Irishman on the swim with me. Then seconds before the cannon went off the PA started to blare the intro to U2's 'Where the Streets Have No Name' and, cheesy as that sounds, it sent me into overdrive. Hearing that organ intro and then The Edge's guitar as the cannon went off got me through the water before you could say 'seals'.

I flew through the swim, no problems, calm and centred and dare I say it, having fun. When I got out of the water I noticed one of our crew, Ian, a gent of a man, white as a ghost at the side of the lake. Poor guy had swallowed too much water in the swim and had to pull out. He was very lucky but it gave me an awful fright. The only real issue I faced was that I was bursting for a pee and because I was welded into a wetsuit there was no chance of it. It was all that went through my head, apart from my mental soundtrack, 'Sunchyme'.

Getting onto the bike for the 90km time trial was an incredible experience. The crowds were roaring and pushing us on. On the cycle even though you are pushing yourself to the limit you can't help but take in the beauty of the Austrian countryside. We cycled parallel to the Danube and through the blackish-green valleys of Austria, surrounded by miles of forest. My personal jukebox changed tune from Dario G to 'The Hills are Alive with the Sound of Music', not surprisingly. At about 60km we hit a 10km mountain climb that was tough as hell. All I kept thinking about was Gerry Duffy's mantra, 'We get to do this.' I got off the bike feeling strong, if incredibly sunburnt, and made my way out onto the run course. Once again, Derry, my friend who supported me through my first triathlon, ran beside me at the other side of the fence in a pair of jeans and with a big bag. The poor bollix must have been chafing to bits but it shows the character of the guy and his friendship, there to get me through.

Seeing the Irish flags being waved by some of the supporters was like a shot of pure adrenaline as I made my way around the half-marathon course. I had an unmerciful pain in my stomach at this stage and was red rare with sunburn but it was something I had never felt before. As I made my made way to the finish line a wave of emotion ran through my body. Spectators rose up in cheer along the 'ironman mile'; some girl even threw a tricolour at me. I wanted to cry but I knew there were pictures at the end so I thought it advisable to hold it together. I started to slap my legs to thank them for getting me through the race. Only I had known the long journey I had to make to get here, and now it was just me and Jeffrey finishing the race. I thought of some of the less happy things I had been through. To the punter watching, it was just some big guy delighted he had finished; to me it was a defining moment in my life. Roz and the other guys were waiting for me as I crossed the line. I immediately embraced her, she knew all too well why this moment meant so much to me, and it was amazing to share it with her.

14. A band of brothers

THE MORNING AFTER THE RACE, I got out of bed and could barely walk to the toilet. I had never known muscle pain like it; I was walking like John Wayne after getting a kick in the arse with a pair of steel toe cap Doc Martens. The sunburn on my back and shoulders was so bad that the sheets from the bed had stuck to me. I could not sit down because the muscles in my backside were so sore, I could not stand up because my lower back was rigid-tight like granite and I could not lie back down as we had a flight to catch and I knew that if I even put my head down again, I'd be going nowhere. But for all that, mentally, I felt amazing. I had allowed myself that moment of self-compassion as I woke up to the day; I was exploding with gratitude and a deep-seated positivity that overcame every ounce of physical pain I was in.

On the flight home, following through on the whole self-compassion vibe, I managed to demolish an entire industrial-size bar of Toblerone.

The week following the race I took a complete rest from any form of training, to allow myself to recover. I was worried that if I did not exercise it might play out negatively in my head but my brain knew my body needed to rest. This close-knit bond between the mind and body understands the need for complete rest after such a tough challenge, so I did something I rarely do, I took a week off.

Jeffrey wasn't going to adapt to this new lifestyle that easily. Over the next few weeks I noticed a pretty intense fluctuation in my moods. There would be days that a shadow could come over me suddenly and for no apparent reason, and I would become incredibly anxious. If I was watching a film or a TV show or reading about something bad that had happened I would start to panic. My sleep patterns became increasingly disturbed, while I became easily irritated or distracted. It was almost impossible to focus on anything and my motivation levels dropped dramatically.

You'd think I would have learned from past experiences. I did not see this crash coming, I had presumed that I was so far on in my recovery that I didn't need to even consider such crashes after such highs, and it annoyed me intensely that I had allowed myself become so naive. Recovery is ongoing and requires constant work and awareness, and I worked so hard towards a goal that when I achieved it, I did not know where to go next. Some people say 'Enjoy the moment' or 'Have a break now' but the notion of quitting something early on drummed up an even more competitive spark in me, to defy the very thought of it. I know my body and my mind and I should have thought of this congenital restlessness leading up to the event.

And so Jeffrey returned to wield his influence and bully my mind. Over the next few weeks the two of us really were not getting on. And I was being an arsehole to everyone around me. I knew what I had to do to move on but I could not easily motivate myself to do it. For me, these are the moments when you have to define and create your own motivations; waiting for someone else to do it is a waste of time and also deeply frustrating.

Being aware that I was low allowed me to make certain decisions to limit the effect. I avoided alcohol completely, I kept my diet as nourishing as I could, but I did find it hard to exercise. I had been so strict on myself leading up to the ironman that my body was almost rebelling against that discipline. Each time I crash like this it allows me gain more knowledge of my mind and of how Jeffrey operates, it allows me to make decisions for the future that keep my recovery on track. I knew why it was happening but that did not stop me wanting to lose the head some days. It almost felt as if I were in a constant state of panic, not quite a panic attack but I had to fight for every breath, every hour of the day. It was exhausting. I really considered going back on medication, even procuring sleeping tablets, as some days it felt as if that control I had fought so hard to rein back into my life was slowly slipping away again. This is the nature of mental illness: yes, I was much stronger than I was in the past, but that does not mean I won't have to deal with problems in the future. The difference is, I now hope to face these problems in a much more understanding and accepting society, while armed with coping mechanisms.

One evening I was feeling seriously uncomfortable in my own skin. I could not sit still for longer than a few seconds and my mind raced at an uncontrollable pace. I kept pulling my hair and there was the familiar anxiety, like acid in my chest and stomach. At times like these the Darwinian approach kicks in and I go into survival mode, locking down and away from people to allow myself to get through it. Not an ideal technique but it's the one that makes it easiest on me. I do not try to be positive, I do not try to pretend that meditation can help me in this acute phase. I just have to batten down the hatches and allow it move on, and recall that it's okay to feel like this every now and again. It's normal, and the sooner you accept it and let it happen, the sooner it passes.

But it wasn't easy. I was panicking so much that I forced myself to vomit, aggressively trying to rid myself of the anxiety that was crippling my gut. I could not catch my breath as I lay over the toilet to throw up and I felt as if I was going to melt with the heat. It wasn't even a panic attack, it was just like one long period of intense uneasiness that took over my entire body.

It's often the case that when my anxiety penetrates this deep I get extremely low, and typically, that's what happened next. I am not sure my depression is born out of the frustration of dealing with anxiety or if each is part of the same condition; either way it's not very pleasant, it robs me of my character and refuses to let me be the person I want to be. I fight for positivity but some days, it's just not in me, and it's on those days that the guilt can take control. You become a pro at avoiding people, not because you dislike them, but because you don't want them to have to endure your moods, you don't want to bring them down with you. I became so blind to all the things that I had learned in the past, all the coping strategies, all the relaxation techniques. I had exposed myself so much to others that I took the eye off the ball and ignored the warning shots being fired in my own mind.

That August, Roz's sister Rebecca and her boyfriend Mark were doing the ironman in Copenhagen and we had booked a few days over there to lend them our support. I was worried, as given the state I was in, I was not a good person to be around. We were travelling with Roz's other sister Rachel and her boyfriend Stephen who were top-notch people, but I did not want to have to expose my moods to those poor souls when they wanted a few days away for a break and a bit of fun. I tried so hard to put on a brave face but I really did not want to be there, this low and given to snaps of anxiety. I felt guilty that I might be ruining the guys' fun, but tried to find a glimmer of positivity with which to support Rebecca and Mark through their challenge. These are the toughest days, when you have to portray your normality though you feel anything but normal. During the break I would run every morning, eat very well and avoid alcohol – it was €12 a pint in Copenhagen so it wasn't too hard – so I did not add any fuel to the fire. One positive thing was that rather than recoiling in on myself at this time, I informed Roz about how I was feeling and she showed her usual patient and understanding character. But it made the trip difficult.

On the day of the ironman, we got up at 5am to be at the start line to wave off Rebecca and Mark. We had our tricolours and I felt massively proud of Rebecca, who had committed so much to getting to her first ironman. Just months before it had been a world so alien to me. I had never seen myself being involved with something as cracked as this, an intense endurance sport, going incomprehensible distances and at competitive speeds. I was excited for Rebecca and also praying she'd get through it, unscathed and in one piece.

We stationed ourselves at the side of the shore where they were doing a sea swim in a lagoon just 10 miles from Copenhagen. After about an hour I noticed two figures in the distance, a young man sitting on a small raft being pulled by a swimmer, who had two ropes around his shoulder. I was very curious and thought at first that it was just a marshal in the water overseeing the race. I asked a spectator who it was and he informed me that they were twin brothers, Steen and Peder Mondrup. One of them was born with a lack of oxygen and developed cerebral palsy, and was confined to a wheelchair, and here they were, 34 years later, doing an ironman. Steen pulled a small kayak with Peder on it the entire swim course, then cycled the 180km route with him on a custom-made bike, before doing a marathon and pushing his brother in his wheelchair, while Peder had to fight constant spasms to remain upright and make it easier for his brother. That day, Steen crossed them to the finish line in 15 hours. It was truly humbling to watch, a remarkable achievement by both brothers. I would be the first person to say that when someone throws perspective into your face when you are struggling mentally, you want to slap them, but when the perspective arrives unexpectedly, not forced upon you but naturally driven from within, it can really lift you from a dark place.

Seeing those two men that day reignited something in me. It was if that commanding motivation and focus I had got used to had just been hibernating and now it was awakened, fully rested and stronger than ever. Jeffrey was my mate again, I hoped.

Back in Dublin, I felt for the first time in a few months that my mind was a little clearer, and in a better place to assess why I struggled so badly over the summer.

A couple of things became quite evident to me. With all

the training I was doing, all the investment I was putting into improving my resilience and mental fitness, with all the emphasis on consuming the right nutrition and avoiding alcohol, with all the therapies I practised, from CBT, mindfulness, to a mixed bag of coping techniques, with all the progress I was making with my wellbeing, something was missing.

I need a goal, a target, a destination to aim at. Life has to test me, because when I am tested I am motivated and focused, and when I am motivated and focused I get to use that internal energy that I can't seem to switch off, ever. Over the summer I felt like I was just floating, with no real intentions or goals, and nothing challenged me. This gave Jeffrey time to think, and I don't like it when he has time to think because he often loses the plot and runs away with himself, leaving me for dead in the process.

I am the type of guy who likes to spin many plates at the same time. The reality is I have so many passions and loves that I don't just want to restrict myself to one or two things, but this can lead to scattiness and jumping from one thing to the next without giving either situation enough time or energy. I needed to evaluate where I was in life and what I wanted to do. I had to ask myself the question that I really did not have an answer to when Gerry Hussey asked a group of us almost a year before: what on earth were my values?

Values are what you stand for when you strip back all the trappings people associate with you. Without stripping back, it's very hard to find out who you are. I needed to define my values, to follow them like a lighthouse, guiding me through the darker and rougher days. I needed to understand why I was working so hard to deal with my emotional and mental issues in effective and proactive ways: why I wanted to recover. My values were always overshadowed, always controlled by a higher god, which was my anxiety. I could see more clearly now what was important, and without being tedious about it, I can say those values include compassion, honesty and loyalty.

In the past I had so little compassion for myself it was impossible to care for others. But as I learned to show self-compassion I made the realisation that other people's happiness had a weighty impact on mine. The toxic environments we all find ourselves in can gnaw away at the values we hold dear. Broken trust is a tough wound to heal and with increasing awareness of this I wanted to be trusted, and I wanted to honour and respect that trust, in a world where it's so often cheapened or crushed. I wanted to be a better, more loyal friend, to help carry people close to me through tough times, and celebrate the good times. My family are the accumulation of all my values. They are my core, and their safety and happiness is what drives and motivates me to be the best I can be, and to make them proud. I want Billy to look up to me as he grows older, I want him to grow up in a society that values humanity more than materialistic things, and I want him to be able to reach out to us if he ever needs support, without fear or hesitation.

One thing I knew for sure was that I wanted to try and make a difference to other people. I did not just want to talk about values in the abstract, I wanted to look at ways in which I, along with others, could help bring the conversation to the next step, a step closer to normalising it and a step closer to changing the attitudes in this country towards mental distress and emotional wellbeing.

15. Loving Dublin

ALTHOUGH I HAD BEEN OPENLY speaking about my journey, I still struggled to communicate with complete clarity what went on in my mind. It is still often a struggle. I frequently found myself speaking at schools and universities with great intentions, but the words would get lost in translation, swallowed by emotion and painful memories. It's hard to separate efficient communication from raw emotion. It seems to be a difficult task, to expose yourself, your feelings and emotions while maintaining structure and coherency. Others found it endearing, this no-holds-barred approach, but I found it quite distressing, and I would often return home from delivering a speech on a traumatic subject feeling agitated and anxious. I couldn't detach from the unhappy memories it brought up, even talking about the past can set off that undercarriage of panic. There are legacies that never leave you, you learn to cope and ultimately use them to your advantage, but they can still hang on like a stubborn stain in your life.

There was an internal dilemma I had to overcome. Did I want to park my endeavour to raise awareness and leave it to others, who might have been armed with a better arsenal to cope with the task, or did I want to further venture into the realms of emotional exposure and look at other ways of helping those struggling with their mental health? It was not an easy choice to make but I decided the ball was moving too fast now in the right direction to stop. There was momentum, people were talking, the media were engaging, I couldn't walk away. I just had to look at other ways of communicating the message that complemented and supported my own mental health, and kept Jeffrey content.

I always found writing to be a wonderful therapy for distress. When I allow my thoughts to stay within the walls of my mind and run rampant they can certainly do damage, but when I put these thoughts to paper it removes them from my head to allow space to focus on other, more positive, feelings. I find that writing can be a concise and focused mode of communication, especially when the subject matter is as complex as mental health. When you speak about the subject, emotion can cloud your delivery, your frame of thought, which can lead to a breakdown in communication and incomprehension, but when writing, you are able to assess your feelings and illustrate them more clearly. Writing has also massively helped me to figure out the cost of certain behaviours on my mental health and the benefits of other behaviours. This transparency of thought has been the greatest ally in my recovery. For years I ran away from Jeffrey, failed to recognise his existence, and often when we did engage I was in conflict and aggressive.

That September I set about writing a book, this book, initially as an exercise in self-help, but as I thought about it more I wanted the book to perhaps act as a more articulate and helpful vehicle for what I had been trying to communicate to others. Rather than just speak about my own mental health I wanted to look at ways of highlighting how outdated and damaging the stigma surrounding mental health has been, how I could have got through it much more effectively if I had the coping mechanisms that I have today.

Writing a book about a long-hidden side of your life, where do you even start? I had ceased to drown in my past but looking back, one of my most glaring regrets is how I failed to enjoy and celebrate the unique journey I had come on. This perhaps is the most difficult pill to swallow. That I was constantly fixated on trying to survive, when really I should have triumphed and embraced the amazing opportunities that came my way. I was at times allergic to happiness, and when a glimmer of it flashed into my mind I felt paranoid that it was to be followed by a darkness that never made being happy worthwhile. I was so caught up with the destination that

I somehow forgot to enjoy the journey. I am aware this sounds like a bad country music song and I wish it was just a song, and not 15 years of my life.

I slowly began to map out my 34 years on this planet, checking dates and information about myself. It's remarkable how much data one person can accumulate in 34 years, and funny how I needed to use the internet to find out information about myself but it was surprisingly helpful in structuring my story as I have a porous memory at the best of times. I can honestly say I did not enjoy this experience. As I lined up the dates I realised the number of people I had hurt, the number of opportunities I let slip, and the amount of pain I caused myself over the years, not because I had an untreatable illness but because I lived in a society that made it hard to accept and seek help for this illness. I would not take back anything I did over those years, they have helped me learn so I could grow, so I could be stronger. I just wish I had enjoyed myself, allowed myself to love, and allowed myself to be happy.

Something that also became quite clear to me over the autumn period of 2014 was that my talking about mental health would inevitably become stale for wider society and perhaps the media over time. Not in a negative way, just in a 'Jesus, not that Bressie fella harping on about depression again' kind of way. I get that, so I knew it was important to explore other ways of spreading my message without playing the 'Poor me' card all the time.

I did not just want to talk about it, I wanted to highlight proactive ideas that people struggling could utilise as they were seeking recovery. I wanted to show that there were indeed things that could be done to make the illness less distressing. Due to the complexities of the subject, it was important to start each speech and passage of writing with, 'This is my story', a mental note to stick to what I knew.

It always had to be my story I was telling, in the same way that a singer writes from their heart. Michael Beinhorn used to tell me never to try to write music that doesn't reflect your own experiences or emotions; otherwise the sentiment will be vague or altogether vacant. A good speaker is the same. My story was not one I could easily tart up, so I had to tell it in its rawness and unreserved emotion. Not being an academic or a healthcare professional, I didn't want to convey statistics or policies, or talk about possible solutions. I wasn't trying to tell anybody else's story, I just wanted to normalise the conversation so others perhaps would not be so hesitant in seeking help. I looked at ways of achieving this and it was important to use my experience within the media industry to help magnify my message and the message of others. The media were all too prepared to engage but they required a broader audience interest, understandably.

Next, I set about developing and writing treatments for television documentaries that could perhaps help carry a message in a much more empowering way, but more importantly in a way that ripped apart the stereotypes and stigmas that we largely associate with mental illness in this country. I spent days brainstorming concepts and phoning television producers looking for guidance but in the end I looked at my own journey to help explore some of the various ways people can improve their mental wellbeing.

After a week or so steeped in ideas and concepts I finally came up with a treatment called 'ironmind', fundamentally based around the limit-testing philosophies of ironman triathlons but with its foundations in positive psychology and the well-documented relationship between physical and mental health, a relationship that has been the lifejacket for me for so many years. The documentary would take four people with varying degrees of primary mental health issues, and train them to complete a 70.3 ironman, consisting of a 1.9km swim, 90km cycle and 21km run, consecutively. I wanted to put together an elite team of experts from both the mental health and physical fitness realm and closely assess, monitor and guide them to finishing the race. The emphasis would be on externalising their resilience and developing their coping mechanisms in the obstacles they would encounter.

My aim was to get the documentary on television to put the topic of mental health on the agenda in a very proactive and inspiring way, but this was just the start. I never suggest that physical exercise will unequivocally benefit all people but I certainly believe it is worth exploring, and the research is hard to ignore. Giving yourself a goal and a tough challenge and overcoming it can have a powerful impact on your state of mind. I had an unwavering belief in the 'ironmind' treatment and invested much time in developing it. The story was about a journey of self-discovery, working with resilience and coping strategies to build mental and physical fitness. I am making the documentary with four incredible people who I hope will each leave the experience a stronger, more resilient person. My other hope is that the audience watching, many of whom may not fully comprehend mental illness, will gain a greater understanding of it and that even one individual can become, potentially, a better support link for someone in their life who may be in pain, which furthermore will help reduce the stigma surrounding mental illness.

My next decision was to develop an online presence to help communicate with audiences on a more regular and informal basis. I wanted to create a platform that lent itself to normalising the conversation around emotional wellbeing, that invited people to describe their own personal experiences with their mental health. I did not just want to use information borrowed from experts who even themselves don't yet have a full grasp of depression, anxiety and other psychological illnesses. I wanted people dealing with these from the ground, as it were, to outline how it affects them. The power is in the first-person story, this is what others can relate to, and ultimately it's what offers the most comfort, knowing you are not alone and indeed that there are others out there that understand what it is you are going through.

One of the questions I ask before any of my speeches is 'How many people here actively invest in their minds?' On average no more than five or ten per cent of the room raise their hands, which in today's frantic and hostile world is pretty low. My aim was to educate people in how they could invest in their bodies and minds and help them cope better with all that the world throws at them. I got my ever-supportive mate Derry and his business partner, Pritesh, to build a website that would be a platform for talking about emotional wellbeing. I also wanted the site to offer pragmatic ways of not only dealing with problems but also ways of developing mental fitness every day.

In his book *Outliers*, Malcolm Gladwell suggests that it takes ten thousand hours of practice to achieve mastery in a certain field. I called the blog My1000Hours, which fundamentally suggests that if you invest and dedicate a thousand hours of time to your body and mind you can potentially, with patience, learn to take back control of your life. Everyone's thousand hours is going to be different, it's a subjective journey in which you are the driver. The number is largely irrelevant, just there as an indicator of time. The idea was that the site would highlight all the various options you could perhaps explore, but it wasn't there to give definitive answers. This was up to each individual who came to it and contributed blogs to it, anonymously or publicly.

That November I was invited to speak at a showcase for the popular Irish website lovindublin.com at the Bord Gais Energy Theatre. The event was a celebration of food culture in Dublin. My initial thought was that perhaps a presentation about mental health from a reality TV show personality might be a tad out of sync with the other speakers, who ranged from world-class chefs to successful entrepreneurs. My concerns were eased when Niall Harbison, LovinDublin's founder, contacted me directly, telling me why he believed this was a good platform to speak about my story and to highlight my vision to a new and perhaps unsuspecting audience. We were starting to produce inspiring success stories in the tech industry in Ireland and sites like lovindublin.com, joe.ie, entertainment.ie and thejournal.ie were offering Irish audiences a new stream of media to compete with print, radio and television. I had a message and wanted to magnify that message to reach as many people as possible, and knew that this perhaps could help get that message to more people. If even one person benefited from it, that would be enough for me.

I wasn't nervous in any way about the speech until a few days before the event when I started to see all the online activity surrounding it. The retweets, the Facebook shares, the visible buzz it was creating. I noticed some people questioning why I was speaking at the event, with one not-so-supportive tweeter saying, 'I hope that long string of piss doesn't start talking about singing, or how he used to play rugby.' To be fair it was almost a factual observation: I am indeed long, and inclined to mention singing and rugby when I speak publicly. I received a call from the event organisers informing me that I had 18 minutes on stage, which unnerved me as I had never been timed when doing my speeches and also I was unsure whether I could communicate my message effectively in that time. Louise on the phone assured me that I would not be pulled off stage or anything, it was just a guideline (perhaps a safety net also, in case the speech was a car crash).

It was in the days leading up to the speech that I truly noticed a progression in my ability to deal with these types of situations. I practised my relaxation techniques, which at this stage were well-oiled machines that could regulate and support me through any situation. At one time, getting up in front of two thousand people and literally laying everything on the line emotionally, exposing myself and my past in its rawest form, would have torn me apart with anxiety, sleepless nights and stress, but by now I had failed enough, I was prepared. I accepted that if emotion got the better of me then I would just let it happen. The one thing that constantly played through my mind was the fact that the event would sway from chefs talking about the art of food, entrepreneurs telling inspiring stories of success, to me, speaking from the doldrums of anxiety and depression. It would be an interesting dynamic, to say the least. It was impossible to predict the audience's reaction but something I have learned through my years of CBT and other therapies is never to stress over things you do not control. A saying prevalent among sports psychologists is 'control the controllable', and right now all I controlled was the ability to deliver my story, in the hope that it could encourage others to seek help and deal with their struggles.

A few days before the event, Niall mailed me to ask would it be okay to film the speech, and once again my initial reaction was caution. I knew that in order to maximise my exposure to what was being said they needed visual content for their sites, but some part of me had thought they would just write a few pieces on what I said rather than show a video. It unnerved me slightly but once again I was able to lean on the techniques that acted like emotional scaffolding for me, and agreed that they could film the talk and then do as they wished with it.

The morning of the speech I woke up with that same ethereal calm I experienced when I spoke to the press about my past for the first time, that gratifying feeling of complete personal acceptance, knowing without hesitancy that this was the right thing to do. On days like this I actively make judgement calls on my behaviours in order to remain calm and focussed. That morning I avoided caffeine, while in the past when I got nervous

I reacted by drowning myself with coffee, a sure-fire way of producing more anxiety. I had discovered the incredibly calming benefits of matcha green tea and on days like this I would drink nothing but this magician's brew. Matcha green tea is bolstered with an amino acid called L-Theanine, which is often referred to as nature's Valium – not the chemical, cotton-mouth inducing kind, but a natural and delicious kind – and it proved to be an incredible mood regulator for me. I avoided foods that were heavy on the digestive system, and I always made sure to exercise in some form on important days like this. So I took myself off for a 10km run and went for an easy swim. Not everybody's cup of breakfast tea, but I have always felt that running in particular can allow you to completely switch off from the world and enjoy the moment and be present. I was calm, relaxed and prepared for whatever was to happen next.

I decided to walk to the Bord Gais Energy Theatre from my apartment, just a short distance away. Arriving, like I always do, ridiculously early for the event, I was greeted by a bevy of personnel, armed with iPads and ear pieces. If I was slightly unsure of how much relevance my speech would have beforehand, I was left in no doubt as to how out of place I was going to be when I saw the entire foyer covered in boutique food stalls and chefs there to promote their brands. This event was aimed predominately at the food industry and I was thrown somewhere in between as some kind of tangent intermission show. Jesus, what have I signed up for? I gazed around in dismay. It was too late now, I was there and had to go for it; if all things failed I could just start talking about my love of a good curry on the stage and hope it resonated with some of these celebrity chefs.

Sitting in the green room before the event, I met the chef Marco Pierre White, a man with a demanding presence. Making polite conversation he asked me, 'What are you speaking about this evening?' I surprisingly and without hindrance replied, 'Depression and anxiety,' to which Marco retorted, 'Oh, how very uplifting' with a wry but supportive smile, which put me at some form of ease. One of the organisers offered me a beer but I thought better of it; apart from anything I didn't want to have to burp my way through the talk.

I gave myself five minutes alone in the cubicle of the gents toilets before I was called, to regulate my breathing and calm myself down. A chilling clarity occupied my mind, like that feeling you get just as you start to get drunk, when the emotional shield starts to be lowered and you feel content within yourself. I was asked once or twice in the lift on the way to the side of the stage if I was nervous. I informed those people that I was scarily relaxed. I thought to myself, we've come a long way, Jeffrey.

As I waited at the side of the stage to be announced, I could almost visualise what I wanted to say, structured and clear in my mind. Then something horribly familiar happened. As soon as I heard my name being called my brain went to mush, I nearly forgot why I was there. In the ten short steps it took to reach the podium I called with all my might upon my coping mechanisms, to reignite my thought process, allowing myself to take three deep breaths before I spoke: to breathe in the positive energy and breath out the toxic energy, three times, and there was a lot of positive energy in that room.

I am pretty sure no one in that room expected me to say what I said over the coming 20 minutes. I told, as best I could, the story of my struggle with mental health, sometimes stumbling over the painful parts. As the speech progressed I managed to control my emotion. Sometimes when I feel emotional I start to curse in order to counterbalance the emotion and that's exactly what happened, expletives flew off that mic. My mammy will be raging with me, I thought to myself. While I was speaking to this largely young graduate audience I witnessed girlfriends embracing their boyfriends, comforting each other, I saw friends holding the hands of their friends, I saw parents on the brink of tears. Quite simply, I witnessed people being human. I wasn't alone, everyone in this room could directly or indirectly relate to my story but perhaps they felt they could never tell theirs, or the story of their loved ones, due to a stigma we associate with mental illness that is ingrained in our society. There was a special energy in that room and it was an unforgettable moment in my life to see so many people drop their shields and cease to repress their feelings, and I was sincerely grateful to share it with so many people who were so receptive to what I said. One thing everyone in that theatre had in common was that we are humans and no one is immune to pain or designed with an invincible mind.

That evening I walked home through a bitterly cold Dublin city centre, buying myself a bag of chips on the way, drowned in red sauce. It's the simple things. Life moves so fast that we often forget to appreciate those simple moments. They may not be your most defining, but they're the moments when you feel completely at ease with who you are and what you have. I was deeply grateful that evening for the people and the things I had in my life and it felt amazing that I was truly able to celebrate this and really mean it, really feel it with compassion for myself.

Over the next few days I received many mails and messages of support, from people who were at the talk or chatted to those who were there. It was very personally satisfying to know that it was well received and had helped some of the audience. LovinDublin contacted me to say they were editing the talk and putting it online in a day or two and I was innocently unaware of the reaction it was going to have.

I was food shopping in the city when I felt my phone erupt and vibrate continuously in my pocket. When I looked at my phone it was flashing in real time with hundreds of text messages, tweets, Facebook posts, emails. The speech had gone up online and I simply could not believe the reaction it was getting. I talk so frequently about the stigma around mental health and how people judge those with issues, but every last word that was written to me that day was positive and supportive. The internet really is a dynamic place, it was only online 40 minutes and already I could not keep up with the responses. The positive reactions grew and grew and before we knew it the speech had gone viral and various news sites were covering it, but it was the showering of personal reactions I received that really impacted on me. Some of the communications were so honest they were upsetting, yet it was liberating knowing that some people had decided to seek help and open up to loved ones about their illness, an illness that had choked and suffocated them all their lives.

There is one communication I will hold onto. I received a beautiful handwritten letter to my home address in Mullingar from a man in his eighties. He set about telling me that his granddaughter played the video of the speech for him and the family after dinner one evening, as they were all fans of *The Voice*, a family programme. After hearing the speech he turned to his family and for the first time in his life spoke about his depression. A depression he had to hide every day of his life, a depression that never let him be himself, a depression that not only hurt him but many of the people around him. He said how he used to cry himself to sleep while turning his radio up so his family would not hear him, and how relieved he felt that he had now finally told his family. We all have a responsibility in this country not to let anyone go through their entire lives this way. We really have a chance to change this now, and if we do not take this opportunity we will kick ourselves in the arse in a few years when we realise we missed the opportunity. This man, as he said himself, does not have much time left but the time he does have will be a little happier knowing this weighted secret he kept for years is now out in the open.

This felt like the right time to launch my blog, My1000Hours. People were engaging with me online now and I needed a platform to help communicate more efficiently, not just on social media. We set up an email for the site that allowed people to share their stories and it was up to them whether we printed their name or not. Some of the mails we received were seriously inspiring and helped educate me in the other areas of mental health that I wasn't as versed in, such as eating disorders, post-natal depression, obsessive compulsive disorders and bi-polar depression, and I hoped it would help educate our audience on the subject too.

As things were changing and progressing in a positive direction, I was taking care to keep a close eye on my own mental wellbeing. Exposing yourself to so many stories and revelations can be sincerely distressing and at times I could feel that unwelcome feeling of panic and anxiety sweep over me. But I kept talking to others, sharing the load with people I trusted, and I found the Headspace app, a mindfulness app with relaxation techniques, to be a lifesaver on many occasions. The ability to meditate in the midst of all the madness was a practice I had to dedicate a lot of time to but it really has become the gift that keeps on giving.

I sensed this roller-coaster few months was just the beginning of something much more profound and I was excited to be a part of it, even if Jeffrey was coming with me.

16. Run your life

ROZ AND I SPENT THE 2015 New Year in the breathtaking surroundings of Ashford Castle in County Mayo. Sitting by the baronial fireplace having a drink, going clay pigeon shooting and cycling through wild Connemara was a universe away from the usual festivities – three-hour queues to get into nightclubs while some girl screams into your ear after five bottles of Blue Wicked that she hates your band, or *The Voice*, or what have you. 2014 was without doubt a test of my emotional endurance, a year when I exposed myself emotionally to so many people but also a year when I accepted the realisation that recovery from my condition would take constant focus and an extensive effort, and also a touch of selfishness. I could not afford to believe for one second that I was clear of the suffocating grasp of general anxiety disorder. Jeffrey had weakened his grip no doubt, but every now and again, when he got pissed off, he wielded all his smothering strength.

I have become meticulously observant of how Jeffrey works. At times this focused awareness has made me overanalyse and scrutinise every behaviour, every mistake and every decision I make, so I've had to decipher the difference between what in CBT they call internal self-awareness – awareness of ourselves – and external self-awareness – how we believe others perceive us. How others perceive us is hypothetical and shouldn't matter, it's how we value ourselves that matters. Giving a name to my anxiety and depression in Jeffrey, and getting to know him as a friend, promoted my internal self-awareness which led to more astute and positive decisions for my emotional wellbeing. But over-emphasis on my external self-awareness led to unnecessary worry of what other people thought of me – it made me worry about things that I did not control.

Looking back, the year had highlighted for me just how many people are affected by varying kinds of mental health issues. For all my disgust at the lazy stereotypes often associated with mental illness, I found myself shocked by some of the people informing me of their mental distress. Friends, peers and colleagues I viewed as living the perfect lives, having amazing jobs, relationships, family and health, told me about how they felt the constant need to disguise their dark days, their sleepless nights and horrific panic attacks. I was pissed off with myself for labelling them as superhuman: after everything I had been through I was still a product of the senseless stigma, boxing off people in relation to their material worth and superficial appearance. I concluded that the most creative, talented, kind, ambitious, intelligent, honest, successful people I know are people living with a mental illness of some degree. Sure there will be days when they can't demonstrate the resilience and emotional intelligence they undoubtedly possess, perhaps as a result of knowing so well what it is to be vulnerable, but it's there.

The ups and downs of the year also steeled me with some of the clear objectives I wanted to achieve over the coming years, around changing attitudes in Ireland towards mental health, through the media, through interaction and conversation but more profoundly and strategically through our education system. Our teenagers are part of an uncontrollably progressive and dynamic society, pitted straight into an information age that even adults struggle to keep up with. They are being accosted by unrealistic and fictional standards of how they should look and be, as portrayed in both digital and mainstream media. They are finding themselves exposed to juggernauts of information and misinformation on a daily basis, having to deal with emotional issues far beyond what their young age has equipped them for.

We have a fundamental responsibility to prepare our teenagers for what they have to face, and I feel this personal development needs to be prioritised in our education system above all other areas. I put a team of professionals together that would allow me to spearhead a campaign to see how we can first help train all our teachers in emotional wellbeing, not only for the benefit of their pupils, but for themselves. During our meetings we looked at ways of placing mental wellbeing in the curriculum with the aim of promoting human development alongside academic achievement. We wanted to educate people not in a goal-oriented, box-ticking way, but in a meaningful and sustainable way. I know this will take a while, and patience is critical, but I feel very passionate about the need for change in our education system without making it a political war, and am willing to wait. I hope we can all work together on this.

In those early months, I was asked to put a piece together for a current affairs debate on RTÉ 1 regarding mental health concerns in our schools and building resilience in our teenagers. On the show a handful of teachers argued that it's not their job to be therapists or counsellors, while politicians argued with union members about cuts and other issues. I thought to myself, why can't we just park this politics and leave behind egotistical concerns, and put humanity first? If we all care about our younger generations enough then we can find a way of making this work. I finished my short slot on the show by saying that I didn't want to look back on this in five years and see an opportunity to make a difference lost.

Parents of kids in primary schools are now reporting levels of anxiety in their children unseen before. It is unsurprising, given young children's exposure to so many gadgets and forms of technology, often a kaleidoscope of photon screens. I have spoken with mothers whose children as young as eight lie awake at night, experiencing panic attacks and worrying about their appearance. Kids at that age are hard-wired to be present, not to think too much of the past or the future, but to just revel in the now. When I was eight I was wondering if it was okay to eat worms, my only worry being whether my tree fort would still be there in the morning. No kid should have to live with anxiety or depression and it's at this age they might be most receptive to coping strategies such as mindfulness.

On one occasion I was geared up to speak to a group of primary-school kids. Just before I went into the first classroom, the principal asked me with evident concern what I was planning to talk about. She asked me would I be speaking about depression or suicide or other mental health issues. I assured her that I was not going to engage in that type of conversation with these kids, who ranged from baby infants to sixth class.

The first question I asked the kids was, 'Do you ever get scared?', to which they nodded in unison. I then asked them, 'Do you ever get a little bit sad, say if your mum is going away for a few days and you miss her, or something frightened you?' Of course, every kid put their hand up, quick to inform me of the various things that make them sad or scared. 'Mummy and daddy fighting,' one young boy screamed, much to the visible embarrassment of his parents who were sitting at the back of the hall. One kid hilariously roared, 'I get scared when I watch *EastEnders* with me ma,' which I immediately related to, having been exposed on a few occasions to that soul-destroying soap. It's a hard watch.

'Okay,' I said, 'now I want to teach you a little trick that can help you feel better when you are sad or scared. I want you all to close your eyes, and think of the happiest moment you can remember in your life. It could be your first trip to Disneyland, or it could be your last birthday party. Try and remember everything about that moment, the weather, who was there, everything you can. Now when you have the moment clear in your head, I want you all to take ten very deep breaths in and out, and squeeze your thumb and forefinger together on each hand as hard as you can. After ten breaths, open your eyes and release your fingers.

'Now, every time you feel scared or sad, all you need to do is squeeze your thumb and forefinger together like this.' I showed them this empowering technique I had learned through CBT, hoping it might serve them at some point.

Their eyes lit up, they could not believe that all they had to do was squeeze their fingers together when they got scared or sad, and it might calm them. To us it would seem too simple to fall for immediately, but to kids it was like a magic trick. I thought to myself that day, if we introduce techniques like these in our primary schools, like a handful of schools are already doing, our kids will have developed functioning mental fitness habits by the time they enter into secondary education, far more equipped to deal with their emotional wellbeing.

The New Year is a strange time for us all. Some see it as a new start, a personal renaissance, while others take it as an arduous punishment for December's excesses, and often struggle both financially and mentally. We set ourselves ambitious resolutions but often forget to establish our values or motivations for doing so, and hence many of us fail to maintain our goals. Feeling guilty because you ate 12 tins of Roses and drank half an off-licence over the festive period is normal, but if we put ourselves through a sudden and severe detox come 1 January we're destined to fail, if we don't dig deeper for motivation.

My resolutions were built around the idea of further bolstering my resilience and mental fitness. It worked for me to examine areas that I felt I could improve on psychologically without drastically changing my lifestyle, my motivation. I wanted a better life so I could be a better person, both for myself and my loved ones. I had just achieved a first in semester one of my sports psychology certificate, which gave me a massive lift. The knowledge I had personally gained through my life had transferred to academia. I was deeply passionate about learning more about how people's brains really work so threw myself into the second semester with enthusiasm, enrolling to do a master's degree in the subject. Having versed myself thoroughly on the benefits of the positive psychology movement, I set a number of structured guidelines for myself for 2015.

Firstly, I wanted to limit my exposure to toxic environments. Places where I could not be myself, or felt that others were not being themselves. The entertainment industry is not renowned for promoting authenticity and depth in its personalities. It is an insecure industry, where position hangs on popularity, and that creates insecurity in people. Fakeness and bitchiness are core ingredients of a toxic environment, and although it's hard to totally avoid these situations, I wanted to actively try to keep away from them. If I walked into a room and heard people ripping someone's character apart – you would be amused at how often it happens in TV and in music – I decided not to engage with it, or to quite simply walk out.

Secondly, I wanted to continue practising self-compassion, nurturing the ability we all have to show some love for ourselves and pride in ourselves. I wanted to discover at least one thing a day for which I could show self-compassion. In that five minutes just before falling asleep at night, I could quietly congratulate myself for doing something well that day. It did not have to be any profound or noble deed, just something as minimal as making somebody a cup of tea, or going for a run when it was the last thing I wanted to do. By showing self-compassion I was letting my brain shut down slowly on a positive note, ending my day the way in which I wanted to start the next day.

Thirdly, when I woke up, before my eyes even opened, I would say 30 silent 'Thank yous'. I would show gratitude for all the things I have in my life, from the most simple things like a bed and toothpaste, to the more substantial, like family, friends, a roof over my head.

Today, by nurturing and practising this, I define which way I want my day to go. My mind embraces the day rather than resenting it. Gerry Hussey, a man who speaks with refreshing clarity on the subject of mental health, once told me, 'You could wake up on the most beautiful desert island, with warm sand under your back, overlooking endless blue seas, with the gentle calming noise of the waves on the shore, and you could stand into a bucket of shit.' As someone with a propensity to mishap, the phrase stuck around with me.

My next daily goal was to practise 30 mindful moments. Small, short moments throughout the day when I actively became present, allowing a brief break for my overworked mind. You do not have to be in the lotus position in a remote Buddhist sanctuary to practise mindfulness, it can be done at any point in the day. When you are having your first cup of tea in the morning, you can feel its warmth going down your throat and into your stomach, and note the comfort of it. When you are standing in the rain, feel the contact of the water on your skin, embrace it, recognise it. When you are walking home from work, be aware of the air you are breathing, let it fill your lungs. Breathe in positive energy and breathe out toxic, negative energy. For me, doing this was like massaging my mind for a few seconds' break from the chaos of everyday life.

Finally, I wanted to make an extra-special effort to stop judging others. I came to the realisation that automatically judging other people eventually made me deeply anxious. In the past, if I found myself going on a rant about someone, tearing their character apart for no other reason but to nurture my own insecurities and jealousy, I would get an acid feeling in my stomach and would become anxious and panicked. I wanted to become more aware of this, and seek the best in others, however irredeemably nasty they seemed in a moment in time. It allowed me to concentrate more on myself and less on others, and control what I can control.

By putting these together, and sticking by them routinely, along with the other therapies and practices I chose, I could regulate my mental health in a way that was enjoyable and fulfilling.

There is a science behind all these points too. When we are compassionate, or show gratitude, we emit neurotransmitters that make us feel good, calm, happy. When we judge others, or surround ourselves with toxic people, we emit the stress hormone cortisol, which makes us feel anxious, stressed, or low. For me, being instinctively cynical about treatments and therapies, learning the scientific angle made the word 'self-aware' easier to grasp and comprehend.

Do not get me wrong, I still had internal conversations with Jeffrey. But our relationship changed from a combative one to a pleasant one. Jeffrey became more like a good friend who had gone travelling for a while and come back a different man. We touched base every now and then, and when he returned we embraced each other's foibles and even enjoyed each other's company. You could say we were not growing apart, we had been through so much together.

Throughout the early months of 2015 I put together the My1000Hours run for early March in the Phoenix Park in Dublin, in conjunction with the *Irish Independent*. The newspaper gave us an editorial for eight weeks leading up to the run, which I wrote along with Gerry Hussey and our running coach Mark McCabe. Each week leading up to the run we put the running programme in the paper, but more importantly, myself and Gerry got to write about mental fitness and coping strategies, all the time helping to normalise the conversation around mental health in Ireland. This was an opportunity to reach a vast audience and was exactly why I set up the service My1000Hours in the first place. The focus of the editorial was on training, but also on highlighting issues and building people's resilience through the eight-week programme.

When we first spoke with the *Irish Independent*, our aim was to get 1,500 runners on board. We wanted to build the relationship going forward so we could help grow our audience and reach more people. It became quickly evident we would surpass this target as the interest in the run erupted. It came from people who had never run before, people looking at ways of building their holistic fitness, their bodies and minds, who wanted to engage with exercise without the fear factor, which we removed from the equation. Our editorials were aimed at empowering people by offering coping strategies and resilience advice. This was about a community of people coming together and looking at ways of taking back control of their lives, and it was amazing.

In the weeks leading up to the run, the numbers grew and grew. Small rural areas were putting together groups of participants, not only to get out and exercise together, but more importantly to get out and talk to one another, open up and support each other, emotionally and physically. It grew organically and people were grasping the vision that I had when I started this project.

On the morning of the run, Derry, my partner in My1000Hours, picked me up from my apartment. We were both nervous and quite emotional at the idea of driving up to the park to see a mass of people in My1000Hours t-shirts. It was a beautiful dry day and I could feel the positive energy from the minute we drove through the gates of Phoenix Park. The event organiser had just texted Derry to inform him that the final figure for those entering the run was close to 4,500. My jaw dropped. As runs go, this was off the charts, no one expected that many. I could not believe my eyes when we pulled up to the starting area inside the park, where the road was closed to allow for a long corridor of people. There were families and friends there to support the thousands of runners. I met my family, who were all running, a very special moment. I lifted up my nephew Billy, who is a beacon of brightness in my life and who I love dearly. People were milling everywhere in sight, rushing up looking for a photo or to have a chat. Despite the size of the crowd I felt no inkling of panic; I felt electric, every part of me was taking this in. I can say with certainty that I felt happy to the very core of myself.

With thousands of people around me it was hard to envisage the impact it was having on anybody individually, but this changed when I was called aside by an elderly man, perhaps in his early seventies. He asked could he speak to me for a moment. He was a short man, with a slightly bent-over back, a thick rural accent. I noticed he didn't tell me his name. Not making eye contact, he said quietly that he was here to do the 5km run. He had heavy, tired eyes.

He proceeded to inform me of how he had not been able to leave his house for years. He lived alone, and struggled alone, and disguised his condition from everyone in his small rural village in the west of Ireland. Looking at me directly now, he told me that a neighbour, having heard of this run and what it was about, called to his house one evening to ask would he walk with her once or twice a week and perhaps consider doing the 5km event in March. He started walking out with this neighbour each week, where they would talk about life, their health and their emotions; soon other neighbours in the area joined them. This man who believed he was alone and totally isolated realised that he had a community of people willing to support him, but also a community of people who have had to endure similar struggles themselves. He came up on a bus hired by the people in the village to do the run, and they had organised a get-together and a party back home for when it was over. He shook my hand, and I could see a tear in the corner of his eye.

On that run, as we cut through the park I spoke to people openly, about things that were once so secret to me but never needed to be. Families and friends watched as their loved ones ran ahead, shouting chants of encouragement. That evening, after everyone had congratulated themselves on a successful day, I went home and sat on my couch. I allowed myself some time to experience the gratitude of knowing there was a man on a bus travelling back home west, whose life was now in a better place.

17. Limping home

YOU MIGHT ASK WHY SOMEONE would voluntarily put themselves through a 70.3 ironman, consisting of a 70-mile (about 113km) swim, cycle and run through varying terrain under a beating sun. For me, training towards such a foreseeable goal in the company of like-minded people is a pleasure and a privilege that is inextricably bound to my recovery. The alternative of sitting at home is not an option. In the months leading up to the race in August I felt good, I felt strong, I felt happy. I noticed big leaps in my progress and found I was able to enjoy the journey, without heaping pressure on myself to get to the destination.

Alongside competing in the event, I was also starting to film a documentary called *Ironmind*, a story based on the connection between physical and mental resilience, which would bring four people towards a 70.3 ironman later in the year. Now I had persuaded others to join me on the journey, I was determined to give it everything I had.

As the summer months approached, I focused more
and more on my training, both mentally and physically.
Although I was a professional rugby player for many
years, this was the strongest, fittest, most clear-sighted I
had ever felt. Unlike in that unwittingly self-destructive
time, I was now looking after my body in every way.
My diet was good, I was filling myself with the proper
nutrients to help sustain my training programme. I was
getting faster and stronger on the bike, I was running for
hours on end and barely breaking a sweat, and where once
the swim was my arch-weakness, it had now become my
strength. I almost felt invincible and I embraced this idea
with every bit of ambition I had. I allowed myself 30–40
minutes a day to work on my mental fitness, starting
with mindfulness, and the visualisation and relaxation
techniques that I can access freely at any moment. It felt
like I had total control over my body and mind, give
or take the odd down day, which is totally normal and
expected when you live with anxiety.

One morning I got a call from the Scottish tourist
board asking me would I be interested in cycling around
Scotland to promote tourism in the region. My mother is
from Glasgow and my sisters and brother all live there
now, so there is a strong connection. I couldn't say no to
an opportunity to cycle around one of the most beautiful
places in the world and jumped at the chance, persuading
my mates Eoghan and Liam to come along. The tough

Scottish highlands were ideal cycling ground to build some extra strength leading up to my half-ironman.

The cycle was spectacular, taking in some of the best views of that wild and vast and untainted landscape. On the fourth day, to break the cycle up, we decided to go to an adventure centre and look at a few activities we could do, as we had the morning off. We wanted to give canyoning, or river gorging as they call it, a shot. Essentially, canyoning is getting to the top of a mountain and following the course of a river down it. It involves jumping from a height into deep water, abseiling and rock climbing and it sounded right up my street.

During the safety brief at the bottom of the canyon I was like a child with too much Fanta and Skittles in him. My legs were shaking with the urge to let loose and I was incredibly excited.

We climbed our way to the top of the mountain to begin a welcomed descent; I was exhilarated at the mere thought of it. Although we were wearing wetsuits, the river was piercing cold when we slid down our first group of rocks and plunged into a pool of water 40 feet deep. Steeled, I then jumped off the next small cliff into another pool of water and swam the 30 feet across to our next cliff. Our guide told us that it was extremely important to just step off the next group of rocks, 10 or 15 feet high, into the pool below. If we jumped we could end up in shallow water at the edge of the pool, but if we stepped, there was a relatively small margin of error. I'm not sure where my mind was when the guide was informing us of this. I figured that whatever was being said, he was being needlessly cautious and so I continued my descent, caught up in the sheer buzz of canyoning.

Here my unerring propensity for injury snapped back into action. I was soon to land myself in another avoidable situation that perhaps, in hindsight, had a message attached that went something along the lines of: slow down. As I made my way down off the rocks, my instincts made me jump slightly out from the small cliff. Even if I had listened to the warnings, it wouldn't have felt right to step carefully when presented with what seemed like a bottomless pool of beautiful ice-cold water.

The guides were waiting beneath us and mid-flight, I could see the terror in their eyes. It became immediately evident that I had jumped too far, as I saw a large slab of rock just below the surface of the water. As I made contact with the water I knew I was in for it. Both my feet made direct impact with the rock below the surface, as the full weight of my sixteen-stone frame, jumping from a height, drove my toes up to my shins, and bent my ankles over themselves. The pain shot up through my hips and into my back, my ears rang with shock. I pulled myself onto a rock, signalling to my guide and Eoghan that something was seriously wrong. I could not bear any weight. I was sure I'd heard a snap on impact with the rock, and believed I had broken both my legs. As I lay on the rock, I remained completely, scarily calm, while our guide tried to work out how we could get back out of the gorge. We couldn't keep going down as this involved more jumps and abseiling and my legs weren't up to it. I was in agony. The only way out was by helicopter or making our way by somehow climbing back up the rocks and cliffs.

Now, I wasn't opting for the helicopter. If my legs weren't broken, I would have felt like an awful eejit. I would not have lived down a dramatic rescue operation if I ended up with just a sore ankle. I decided to try and make it out by crawling, and using my upper body strength to pull myself with the abseil ropes up the rocks. The guides were utmost professionals, the kind of people you want near you in a crisis, and soon we came across three experienced canyoners who recognised the emergency and helped me make my way out, working a path up the easier part of that treacherous vertical ascent.

The pain of climbing those rocks was really something. It pulsed through my legs and made me feel faint at times. I thought back to my early open-water swim days and started to sing in my head Dario G's 'Sunchyme', to try and stay calm, in between the occasional groan of pain. Anxiety wanted to engulf me but the simple refrain of that song had a strange power to keep it away, to remind it who was boss here. My legs would hit off the rocks and with each impact I felt nauseous with pain, but soon we were making progress. With the help of those around me, I managed to make it to the top of the gorge. The five canyoners we had met carried me aloft on a 'queen's lift', arms criss-crossed underneath me, down the mountain to the safety of the jeep, where we called the ambulance. I had been in this situation many times before but now, I had to succumb to the help of others, to lie back and relax as these kind people carried me the last part of the way. It was secretly almost enjoyable: a hamlet cigar moment. The ambulance could not get access to the mountain so instead, we had to drive our car down the mountain with me in the boot and my legs hanging out. That was less of a hamlet cigar moment.

Having eased me into the ambulance in my damp wetsuit, the paramedic told me it was possible that I had broken my left leg and perhaps dislocated my right ankle, before she stuck a mask with laughing gas around my mouth to ease the pain. I am pretty sure I finished the canister within five minutes. I remained calm even though I could see that some of the guys were seriously concerned. Liam, who had cleverly given canyoning a miss, met us at the ambulance, visibly upset. I am an intensely guarded person, because of the way I grew up. I have only a handful of people I call close friends, and Liam is one. He has been through tragedy in his life, and we have worked through a lot together. He knew what a vast effort I had put into my training, and I could tell he was worried more for my mental state than my physical.

I really wondered, lying in that ambulance, was injury almost a form of self-expression to me? I never half-did anything. If I was going to get injured, I was going to get injured – I wasn't going to get just a little hurt. I cursed this flaw of recklessness, but resolved not to blame myself for things beyond my control. In situations like this, my default setting used to be severe depression and spiralling anxiety. This time, I was thankful I was okay and in good hands, and I immediately accepted what had just happened to me and understood I would have to move on. There wouldn't be any race in August.

When we arrived in the hospital, the nurse cut me out of my wetsuit as I was by now shivering with the cold, and I was brought down to be X-rayed. It was second nature to me, this radioactive procedure – just going through the motions really.

When I returned, the medics surrounded my bed and I waited for the bad news. As the doctor informed me the leg was not broken, Liam grabbed my arm in relief and, ironically, nearly injured it. The doctor said I had ruptured ligaments in both ankles, which I knew meant a long recovery, but I was grateful it was not a whole lot worse. I lay in the bed and gave myself a few minutes to be upset, to just let it out. I contacted my family and Roz to explain to them what had happened. They seemed to take it worse than I did, knowing how much sacrifice and commitment I had put into the last year, and what that race had meant to me. I knew by the tone in their voices that, like Liam, they were concerned more for my mental health than my ankles. They had seen in the past how something like this could plummet me into the darkness, but I assured them that I was completely fine, a little upset and sore but fine, and full of codeine.

Back in my hotel that night, I lay in bed aware there could be an empty hole in my life now – depending on how I wanted to look at it. And I chose not to feel sorry for myself; I decided that I would fill that hole with something else. Instead of thinking of all the things that I could not do, I thought of the things that I could do. Instead of being angry, I was grateful for all the incredible people I had supporting me. This was not fake positivity I was cultivating to try and counteract the disappointment of the injury when fitness is such a lynchpin of my wellbeing, it was me finding clear and comforting perspective in an otherwise challenging situation. I let myself cry and cry, I didn't suppress the tears. In the tiny hotel room in Inverness, surrounded by melting ice buckets, painkillers and a now obsolete pile of training gear I lay awake all night, writing down ideas, concepts, plans, setting new challenges. I recognised this profound ability to cope, this granite-hard resilience that I had developed over years and years. It amazed me. When my physical fitness let me down, my mental fitness was there to support me and pull me through.

I marvelled again at how this would have affected me ten years ago, how the consequences of losing a pastime so important to me even for a short period did not bear thinking about, back then. I showed compassion to myself for how I had taken back control of my life, little by little. As my loved ones sat at home worrying about me, I lay in bed excited for the future, knowing how strong I had made myself, how strongly I believe that nothing is impossible. Myself and my mate Jeffrey have come a long way together.

When I arrived back in Ireland, feet in casts, on crutches, hobbling from place to place, people would come up to me on the street and in cafes in the centre of Dublin to ask me what had happened. It made me think.

Mental illness doesn't have a limp, we can't see it, so we therefore do not know who is dealing with it, or how much they are hurting. My injury, like most physical injuries, will recover, and I will seek the right guidance and rehabilitation without fear of judgement or isolation, friends and loved ones will get me through it and I will be back on my feet in no time. My hope is that one day mental illness and injury can be put on the same page as physical illness and injury. I hope that people won't fear seeking help, and they will be supported and guided through dark times into the light with those that love them by their sides, and come back stronger and more resilient.

When I got into my apartment, I lay on my couch for hours with my two ankles elevated, constantly icing them and keeping them compressed. I sculpted an environment of positivity, an ideal breeding ground for recovery. I thought of the previous years, when after injury I grew angry, depressed and intensely anxious, where every thought that entered my head was adverse and pernicious, and I was thankful that I had invested so much into my mental fitness and coping mechanisms.

I knew I would have a hole to fill once my beloved race was out of reach. During those weeks of immobility, I rediscovered my intense passion for creativity. I had forgotten what it felt like to sit with my guitar and strum chords, where time becomes irrelevant and you get lost in a melody, almost hypnotised by the amenity of music. I found myself wanting to write songs for the first time in months, years even. There was an internal explosion of creativity that kept my guitar glued to my hands; I found it impossible to put it down. I got taxis to my studio where I was able to work on songs with no distractions, no meetings, no training, and no stress. I felt blessed that when one passion was suppressed, I had another passion in my life, faithfully waiting to take my hand.

This internal energy that flows through my body, once an energy so imperious, uncontrolled and tyrannical, has, with careful, patient and explorative investment, become an assertive ally and impetus for personal and professional development. I have learned to channel and focus this energy rather than control or manipulate it. I challenge myself constantly, remove myself from my comfort zone and drive myself to set and achieve goals, leaning on this energy as a pillar of continuous support.

When I can't cycle, run, swim or go to the gym, I can pick up my guitar, or sit behind a piano, or record in my studio.

I think back to the days when I locked myself in my box room as a reclusive teenager in Mullingar, pretending I was playing on stage to thousands of people, or scoring a try for Ireland in the Six Nations. Days when anxiety became the norm in my life, followed closely by its favourite bedfellow, depression.

Over the years I've wondered about what causes anxiety, whether it is nature or nurture. But very little in the world is black and white, and ultimately I think it's a combination of both. I was lucky enough to come from a loving home, with parents who've always supported me. I was nurtured. Yes, there were worries – my dad being away, the upset it caused. Frightening times in Israel as a young teenager. The way I felt I had to always appear positive as I grew older, as Dad had enough on his plate without a son who was freaking out. I think the seed was there, though – a predisposition to be anxious – waiting for the right triggers to set it off.

I discovered years later, when I finally came clean to Dad about my issues, that he too was no stranger to worry. So perhaps it runs in the family. Mental health issues certainly affect every family in some way, shape or form, and traditionally us men have been the worst at letting it be known. We feel a pressure to put the best foot forward, conceal the cracks.

But of course, it's something that affects every inch of society, bypassing gender, age, race – and we all have a duty to open up the conversation. More often than not, in my experience, when you express what's really going on for you, you find out that people you least expect know exactly how you feel.

A lot has happened since that teenager with the big dreams imagined a different life outside the four walls of a Mullingar bedroom. I got so caught up in the destination that I got lost on the journey. Ultimately, through my own at times challenging reflections, with supportive loving guidance, I came to realise that it's not the destination that really counts, it's the journey. I am a 34-year-old man, and I am going to enjoy the rest of my journey with my mate Jeffrey.

Acknowledgements

THOSE PEOPLE WHO HAVE SHARED their stories with me, inspiring, empowering, harrowing, painful. Thank you sincerely. You have provided me with the motivation to write this book.

Friends and loved ones that stood by me, when so many others would have turned their back, thank you.

At times I struggled writing this book, I really did. I questioned myself, I opened up old scars and returned to moments in my life that, although distressing, ultimately have defined me as a person. I made a conscious decision to surround myself with amazing individuals, to avoid toxic environments and people. To list everyone who has helped me would not be feasible, but the ultimate acknowledgment I can give to you all is that you are no doubt special and deeply important in my life. Thank you.

My publisher Ciara Considine at Hachette, and my literary agent Faith O'Grady, you instilled the belief in me that I could do this, when I truly believed I could not.

Your sensitivity, guidance and encouragement pulled me from many moments of self-doubt and for that I will forever be thankful. Thanks also to Maggie Armstrong for her editing work on the manuscript.

Derry McVeigh and Joanne Byrne, who have helped me to manage my career on top of my work as a mental health campaigner, thank you. You have had to deal with a lot beyond the call of duty, but your passion to help has been unbelievably uplifting and supportive.

To the mental health charities, awareness groups, counsellors and health care professionals throughout Ireland, you are the true backbone of support for those in need in this country when it comes to emotional and mental well-being. Thank you for what you do and the lives you have saved.

To the media, thank you for all the support you have shown me. For too long we have ignored this subject in our media, bolstering an already devastating stigma. Please continue to use your power in a positive light and develop and nurture this conversation.

To everyone who has ever lent a shoulder of support to those that needed it, thank you.